The Golden Gate

THE GOLDEN GATE

Vikram Seth

faber and faber

First published in the United States of America in 1986 by
Random House, Inc., New York and simultaneously
in Canada by Random House of Canada Limited, Toronto

First published in Great Britain in 1986
by Faber and Faber Limited
Bloomsbury House
74–77 Great Russell Street
London WC1B 3DA
Reset in 1999

Typeset by Wilmaset Ltd, Wirral
Printed and bound in Great Britain by
TJ International Ltd, Padstow, Cornwall

Vikram Seth is hereby identified as author of this
work in accordance with Section 77 of the Copyright,
Designs and Patents Act 1988

A CIP record for this book is available from
the British Library

ISBN 978–0–571–21265–1

10 9 8 7 6 5

Acknowledgments

My debts are manifold and various:
First, Stanford University
Where, with progressively precarious
Nurture, my tardy Ph.D.
Has waxed, and waxes, lax and sickly.
Second, to friends who've read this, quickly
Advised me to desist and cease,
Or burbled, "What a masterpiece!"
Or smoothed my steps with sage suggestion.
Third, to John and Susan Hughes
For refuge, friendship, ears, and views.
And, fourth, to you, who did not question
The crude credentials of this verse
But backed your brashness with your purse.

Dedication
to Timothy Steele

So here they are, the chapters ready,
And, half against my will, I'm free
Of this warm enterprise, this heady
Labor that has exhausted me
Through thirteen months, swift and delightful,
Incited by my friends' insightful
Paring and prodding and appeal.
I pray the gentle hands of Steele
Will once again sift through its pages.
If anything in this should grate,
Ascribe it to its natal state;
If anything in this engages
By verse, veracity, or vim,
You know whom I must credit, Tim.

Contents

The Golden Gate

One

1.1   To make a start more swift than weighty,
Hail Muse. Dear Reader, once upon
A time, say, circa 1980,
There lived a man. His name was John.
Successful in his field though only
Twenty-six, respected, lonely,
One evening as he walked across
Golden Gate Park, the ill-judged toss
Of a red frisbee almost brained him.
He thought, "If I died, who'd be sad?
Who'd weep? Who'd gloat? Who would be glad?
Would anybody?" As it pained him,
He turned from this dispiriting theme
To ruminations less extreme.

1.2   He tuned his thoughts to electronic
        Circuitry. This soothed his mind.
        He left irregular (moronic)
        Sentimentality behind.
        He thought of or-gates and of and-gates,
        Of ROMs, of nor-gates, and of nand-gates,
        Of nanoseconds, megabytes,
        And bits and nibbles ... but as flights
        Of silhouetted birds move cawing
        Across the pine-serrated sky,
        Dragged from his cove, not knowing why,
        He feels an urgent riptide drawing
        Him far out, where, caught in the kelp
        Of loneliness, he cries for help.

1.3   John's looks are good. His dress is formal.
        His voice is low. His mind is sound.
        His appetite for work's abnormal.
        A plastic name tag hangs around
        His collar like a votive necklace.
        Though well-paid, he is far from reckless,
        Pays his rent promptly, jogs, does not
        Smoke cigarettes, and rarely pot,
        Eschews both church and heavy drinking,
        Enjoys his garden, likes to read
        Eclectically from Mann to Bede.
        (A surrogate, some say, for thinking.)
        Friends claim he's grown aloof and prim.
        (His boss, though, is well-pleased with him.)

1.4   Gray-eyed, blond-haired, aristocratic
In height, impatience, views, and face,
Discriminating though dogmatic,
Tender beneath a carapace
Of well-groomed tastes and tasteful grooming,
John, though his corporate stock is booming,
For all his mohair, serge, and tweed,
Senses his life has run to seed.
A passionate man, with equal parts of
Irritability and charm,
Without as such intending harm,
His flaring temper singed the hearts of
Several women in the days
Before his chaste, ambitious phase.

1.5   John notes the late September showers
Have tinged the blond hills round the bay
With a new green. He notes the flowers
In their pre-winter bloom. The way
That, when he was a child, the mystery
Of San Francisco's restless history
Kindled in him an answering spark,
It strikes him now as, through the park,
Wrested from old dunes by the westward
Thrust of the green belt to the slow
Pacific swell, his footsteps go.
But it is late. The birds fly nestward
Toward the sunset, and the arc
Of darkness drifts across the park.

5

1.6   It's Friday night. The unfettered city
       Resounds with hedonistic glee.
       John feels a cold cast of self-pity
       Envelop him. No family
       Cushions his solitude, or rather,
       His mother's dead, his English father,
       Retired in his native Kent,
       Rarely responds to letters sent
       (If rarely) by his transatlantic
       Offspring. In letters to *The Times*
       He rails against the nameless crimes
       Of the post office. Waxing frantic
       About delays from coast to coast,
       He hones his wit and damns the post.

1.7   A linkless node, no spouse or sibling,
       No children—John wanders alone
       Into an ice cream parlor. Nibbling
       The edges of a sugar cone
       By turns, a pair of high school lovers
       Stand giggling. John, uncharmed, discovers
       His favorite flavors, Pumpkin Pie
       And Bubble Gum, decides to buy
       A double scoop; sits down; but whether
       His eyes fall on a knot of three
       Schoolgirls, a clamorous family,
       Or, munching cheerfully together,
       A hippie and a Castro clone,
       It hurts that only he's alone.

1.8   He goes home, seeking consolation
        Among old Beatles and Pink Floyd—
        But "Girl" elicits mere frustration,
        While "Money" leaves him more annoyed.
        Alas, he hungers less for money
        Than for a fleeting Taste of Honey.
        Murmuring, "Money—it's a gas! . . .
        The lunatic is on the grass,"
        He pours himself a beer. Desires
        And reminiscences intrude
        Upon his unpropitious mood
        Until he feels that he requires
        A one-way Ticket to Ride—and soon—
        Across the Dark Side of the Moon.

1.9   He thinks back to his days at college,
        To Phil, to Berkeley friends, to nights
        When the pursuit of grades and knowledge
        Foundered in beery jokes and fights.
        Eheu fugaces . . . Silicon Valley
        Lures to ambition's ulcer alley
        Young graduates with siren screams
        Of power and wealth beyond their dreams,
        Ejects the lax, and drives the driven,
        Burning their candles at both ends.
        Thus files take precedence over friends,
        Labor is lauded, leisure riven.
        John kneels bareheaded and unshod
        Before the Chip, a jealous God.

1.10   As did Phil too, until his recent
Flight from the rich realms of Defense
(With what John holds to be indecent
Precipitation and bad sense).
John, still engaged in such endeavors,
Feels Phil's new zest for peace work severs
A thread of mutual interest.
He almost fears to call him lest
Political debate should color
A friendship based on easy cheer,
Light camaraderie, dark beer,
And double-dating. Life's grown duller
Since when—ah, time!—they used to share
The aegis of the Golden Bear.

1.11   He phones Phil, the first time in ages,
But there's no answer. (Friday night.)
He idly thumbs the scribbled pages
Of his address book. Well, he might
Phone Janet Hayakawa. Many
Seasons have sunk since there was any
Hazard a meeting could educe
Their former love. A standing truce
Shelters their friendship from all passion.
They'd felt their union would constrict
Their separate lives. An interdict
Agreed by both, after a fashion
They went about their singular ways,
Slaves to the Chip or artist's daze.

1.12   She is a sculptor. Stress and pleasure
        For her thus perfectly combined,
        The boundaries of toil and leisure
        By definition ill-defined,
        Her worktime doubles as her playtime,
        But hand and eye deployed in daytime
        Yield, when night comes, to ear and hand.
        She is the drummer in a band
        Well known and feared throughout the city:
        The striking sounds of Liquid Sheep
        Rouse distant suburbs from their sleep.
        Unlinked alike to tune or ditty,
        Their music is a throttled yelp—
        Morse crossed with a pig's squeal for help.

1.13   Although such accents supersonic
        Engage her in the fevered night,
        Janet considers it ironic
        That her true forte, try as she might,
        Her quiet forms of bronze and iron—
        Three Eggs, An Adolescent Lion,
        Clothed Nude, Study of Young Man Caught
        In Eagle's Claws—have not yet brought
        The sober critical attention
        She craves. The critics' common nose
        Sniffs magisterially at her shows.
        And as for divine intervention—
        In Schiller's phrase, the very gods
        Strive fruitlessly against such clods.

9

1.14   Blind mouths! They spew their condescension:
Miss Hayakawa, it appears,
Lacks serious sculptural intention.
Where has she been these thirty years?
Are Moore's and Calder's use of medium
Unknown to her? The languid tedium
Of lines too fluid to show pains
Reflect this artist's dated chains:
Derivative, diluted passion,
A facile versatility....
With smooth and blinkered savagery,
Servile and suave, obsessed by fashion,
These chickenhearted chickenshits
Jerk off their weak and venomous wits.

1.15   Though savaged by this vain unkindness
Which she tries not to take to heart,
She too displays unwitting blindness,
Plunging her spirit into art.
Only her cats provide distraction,
Twin paradigms of lazy action.
A short walk from Café Trieste
The three live in an eagle's nest,
A great loft studio, light and airy.
Each day for breakfast Cuff and Link
Have fish to eat and cream to drink.
Their mistress drinks a Bloody Mary
(For inspiration) and devours
Her Weetabix, and works for hours.

1.16   Sweet Siamese of rare refulgence
With chocolate ears and limbs of tow,
Jan gives them love, food, and indulgence.
The cats take this for granted, show
Scant deference to their human betters;
Their baskets woven with gold letters,
In splendor Jan can ill afford,
In silken bed, on sumptuous board
They fatten. Though, when out of favor,
The L and C on their beds are
Interpreted "Louse" and "Catarrh,"
Jan relishes the warmth and savor
The deeds of Cuff and Link confer,
The love they deign to yield to her.

1.17   Through Cuff's exploratory predations
Knobs in electric blankets know
Untimely death. Link's sharp striations
Score the old desk that years ago
Was left by Jan's grandparents, issei,
To her own parents (self-made nisei),
And now (for lack of storage space
In their small flat) stands in this place
Beneath a scroll by her grandfather:
A twilight poem by Wang Wei
He calligraphed that shameful day
In '42: Internment. Rather
Yellowed and frayed in recent years,
This scroll still brings Jan close to tears.

1.18   John stands beside his phone, recalling
Janet's warm beauty, smiling calm,
Her dark eyes, high-boned features, falling
Black ponytail, her vagrant charm.
He thinks, "I guess I'll be the wiser
For talking to a sound adviser."
He dials. To his peeved surprise
An answering machine replies,
Requests his message, name and number.
("Wait for the beep.") John says, "It's me,
John. 234-4963.
No message." Rather than encumber
The brusque machine with his heart's woes,
He wraps himself in pensive prose:

1.19   *Life's Little Ironies* by Hardy,
The gloomier sermons of John Donne,
The *Zibaldone* of Leopardi,
The Queen of Spades. At ten to one,
From the crevasse of melancholy
In which he now is buried wholly,
He hears the phone ring. "Hello, John?
Are you OK? What's going on?
I just got back. I thought I'd phone you
Although it's late. You sounded bad
On the machine, more tired and sad
Than in the whole time that I've known you."
"It's nothing." "Tell you what, let's meet
For lunch tomorrow. 16th Street.

1.20   The Shu Jing. One. It's well-frequented.
Food's great." Next day, not quite at ease,
John shows up early, cologne-scented,
Hyper-immaculate, sits and sees
Families, lovers, inter alia
A circus clown in full regalia,
But as the hope-hour strokes its sum
He fidgets: Janet hasn't come.
Deaf to the pap of Muzak sounding
"O Little Town of Bethlehem"
Anachronistically at them,
The patrons dine with zest. Rebounding
Off plastic chairs and grubby floor
The notes merge with the squeaking door.

1.21   John thinks, "It's not that I'm fastidious. . . .
I wish they'd turn that music down. . . .
It's gross. That calendar is hideous . . .
(He stares at the distasteful clown.)
. . . I've waited half an hour, blast her!"
Her hands encased in clay and plaster,
Janet arrives at twelve to two:
"So sorry, John, I had to do
This torso. Yes, I tried to hurry.
I'm glad you've got yourself a beer.
What's that? Tsingtao? Don't look severe.
I didn't mean for you to worry.
You've ordered? No? This place is fun!
What'll you have? It's family-run."

13

1.22   The food arrives as soon as ordered.
Impressed and ravenous, John relents.
His chopsticks fasten on beef bordered
With broccoli. Enticing scents
Swim over the noise, the greasy table.
Two bottles each of beer enable
Small talk and large, in cyclic waves,
To wash their shores, and John behaves
At last less stiffly if not sadly.
"How are the cats?" "Just fine." "And you?"
"Great." "And the sculpture?" "Yes, that too."
"Your singing group?" "Oh, not too badly.
But I came here to hear your song.
Now sing!" "Jan, I don't know what's wrong.

1.23   I'm young, employed, healthy, ambitious,
Sound, solvent, self-made, self-possessed.
But all my symptoms are pernicious.
The Dow-Jones of my heart's depressed.
The sunflower of my youth is wilting.
The tower of my dreams is tilting.
The zoom lens of my zest is blurred.
The drama of my life's absurd.
What is the root of my neurosis?
I jog, eat brewer's yeast each day,
And yet I feel life slip away.
I wait your sapient diagnosis.
I die! I faint! I fail! I sink!"
"You need a lover, John, I think.

1.24   Someone, I'd say, who's fun to be with—
And, of course, vitamin C to eat—
And choose a richer lens to see with.
Reach for a vision more complete.
Trade in that zoom for a wide angle.
Don't let your drooping sunflower dangle
Its head upon the garden wall.
It needs some watering, that's all. . . ."
The fervor of her declamation
Induces her to drum a roll
With her chopsticks upon her bowl.
A waiter turns in consternation.
". . . Don't put things off till it's too late.
You are the DJ of your fate.

1.25   Think of yourself a few years later,
Possessing, as the years go on,
Less prepossessing vital data:
Love handles . . . ("Thanks a lot," says John.)
. . . Receding . . . (John is getting nervous:
"More rice? I wonder when they'll serve us.")
. . . Hairline . . . ("Funny taste, this tea."
He sips at it distractedly.)
. . . Lonely and lost, sans love, sans lover,
Too much to drink last night . . . (And here
Jan pauses for a sip of beer)
. . . Nursing the dregs of your hangover,
Blubbering into your raisin bran.
Why not do something while you can?"

1.26   "But what?" growls John as this depressing
Directory drums on. "OK,
You've got a point; enough B.S.ing—
Suppose you're right—well, what's the way
To hook chicks?" Angrily and sadly
Jan looks at him. "You'll blow it badly
Till you clean up your Pigspeak act."
"Oh, come now, don't overreact,
Janet, you know I didn't mean it."
"Nor, I suppose, did the crude crass
Hall manager who pinched my ass
Last night. 'Cute chick.' You should have seen it.
I punched his snout. 'To hook a chick'—
Such porcine lingo makes me sick."

1.27   "A venial linguistic tumor."
"It's not benign." "But it was just
A joke, Jan. Where's your sense of humor?"
"It's dormant since last night." "Why must
You blame me for his roving trotter?"
"Because, sweet ostrich, it was not a
Harmless joke. Enough said, John.
You've got my drift. I won't go on."
"I donned machismo just to rile you."
"Well, you succeeded." "Sorry, Jan—
Friends?" "Friends—of course, you fool, how can
You doubt it? Though I think I'll file you
Under 'Male Repentant Pig.'"
John takes her hand, and she a swig.

1.28   "We need first off," says Janet dryly,
       "A venue to begin from." "What?"
       "Your office, John?" she ventures slyly—
       "Any nice women?" "Not too hot."
       "Any nice guys?" "Oh, come on, Janet,
       I just don't go for that, so *can* it."
       "Well, don't knock what you haven't tried."
       John stirs his overstirred stir-fried
       Vegetables for answer, thinking,
       "She's had too much. Should I suggest
       We stop at this one? No, it's best
       To keep the peace. But when she's drinking
       She talks about the weirdest things—
       Guys with guys, or pigs with wings."

1.29   Now Janet's fancy (wingéd? flighty?)
       From pigs to pictures is enticed.
       "Ever tried seeking Aphrodite
       In a museum?" John cries, "Christ!
       Haven't I just? With base volition
       I've gaped at Goya, ogled Titian,
       Loitered by Rubens with intent,
       But have (to date) not made a dent
       In the cool academic armor
       The women wandering through those halls
       Assume; we stare at paint and walls
       But not a word's exchanged." Then, calmer:
       "I gave it up eventually.
       My weekends mean too much to me."

1.30   "Your weekends—well, how do you spend them?"
        John thinks—where do my weekends go?
        "Oh, things go wrong. I have to mend them:
        A plug, the plumbing, the Peugeot,
        A stone stuck in the electric mower—
        And I'm a regular moviegoer:
        Whenever there's a decent show
        I try to make the time and go.
        Last week I saw a Buster Keaton.
        (I think he's great. He never smiles.)
        Then home, to catch up on my files.
        A can of chili. When I've eaten,
        The late night news, and so to bed."
        John looks forlorn as this is said.

1.31   "I guess my weekends aren't too sprightly
        After all." Jan with a kiss
        ("Poor little rich boy") murmurs lightly,
        "We've got to put a stop to this.
        There has to be a swift solution
        To this impasse." "Electrocution?
        I could jump off the Golden Gate.
        I read in the *Bay Guardian* . . ." "Wait!
        I've got it, John! The perfect answer!
        I should have thought of it. My friend—
        Your sufferings are at an end."
        "That sounds as terminal as cancer.
        Let's hear it." With a tame surmise
        He listens. Jan says: "Advertise."

1.32   "What? Advertise? You must be joking!"
        "I'm serious." "Jan, you're nuts." "I'm not."
        "You know, Jan, you've had such a soaking
        In Tsingtao you don't know what's what.
        Me advertise? You must be kidding!"
        "Kiddo, I'm not. Just do my bidding.
        Take out an ad. Right now. Today.
        Young handsome yuppie seeks..." "No way!
        I've always thought your schemes, though wacky
        (Conceived in midair, born in haste),
        Remained within the bounds of taste,
        But as for this one—talk of tacky!
        Let's talk of something else instead.
        Young yuppie...! Better dead than read."

1.33   The family at the next table
        Are listening in with interest.
        "But, John, at least—when you feel able—
        Why don't you put it to the test?"
        "But it's so desperate, so demeaning."
        "Johnny Boy, your mind needs cleaning
        Of the debris of prejudice."
        "Jan, what has that to do with this?"
        "Its definition is," states Janet,
        "Judging a thing before it's tried."
        "But it's the same for suicide,"
        Says John—"or blowing up the planet.
        Why should I try it first to see
        If it agrees or not with me?"

1.34   "But that's ... but that's ..." Janet considers.
        "That's what? It's a meat market, Jan.
        Goats and monkeys, bears, bulls, bidders,
        Buyers: grab me while you can—
        DWJSM, 50,
        Solvent, sexy, thrilling, thrifty,
        Seeks a bosomy brunette
        Who likes to play the flageolet.
        Let me make music with you, baby.
        Box 69. I will not share
        A column with such types out there.
        How could you think I'd do it? Maybe
        You see me as *Male, 26,*
        Who gets his thrills from hooking chicks."

1.35   Janet picks up her fortune cookie,
        Then puts it down, turns to her friend:
        "Don't bank too much on youth. Your rookie
        Season is drawing to an end.
        John, things we would—when young—not think of,
        Start to make sense when, on the brink of
        Thirtydom, we pause to scan
        What salves and salads cannot ban,
        The earliest furrows on our faces,
        The loneliness within our souls,
        Our febrile clawing for mean goals,
        Our programmed cockfights and rat races,
        Our dreary dignity, false pride,
        And hearts stored in formaldehyde.

1.36   Time sidles by: on television
The soaps dissolve, the jingles change.
Defeat or pity or derision
Constricts our hearts. Our looks grow strange
Even to us. The grail, perfection,
Dims, and we come to view rejection
As an endurable result
Of hope and trial, and exult
When search or risk or effort chances
To grant us someone who will do
For love, and who may love us too—
While those who wait, as age advances,
Aloof for Ms. or Mr. Right
Weep to themselves in the still night.

1.37   It's sad to see you look so lonely,
That's all, John." John does not confute
Jan's passionate words. He thinks, "If only
Things were that simple." Moved and mute,
He sits and stares as little bubbles
Fizz in his beer, and his grand troubles
Dissolve: "Well, I'm a lucky man
To have a true friend like you, Jan.
You may be right. But if I do it . . .
Who knows what sort of person I'll
Wind up with." He attempts to smile
But fails. He sighs, "I can't pursue it.
I'm sorry that I'm such a pain.
It simply goes against my grain."

1.38   The family, the clown, the lovers
        Have left. Muttering in Cantonese,
        Impatiently the waiter hovers
        Around the table. "Check, sir?" "Please! . . .
        But, Janet, what have you been doing?
        Last time we met you were pursuing
        A work of deathless interest:
        Sculpting three golf balls in a nest."
        "I'm hunting for an album cover
        For the first disk of Liquid Sheep.
        I know just what I want. I keep
        Remembering this scene: above a
        Meadow of lambs a green and white
        Hot-air balloon is poised in flight.

1.39   Who painted that? Can you remember?"
        "I do, though I can't quite recall. . . .
        Was it the air show last September?
        I think I saw it there, though all
        I know is, it was on a poster
        Sometime last year, well, at the most, a
        Couple of years back. . . . No, I'm stuck.
        Jan, looks as though you're out of luck.
        Afraid my mind's deteriorating. . . ."
        "Oh no, John, no, John, no, John, no!
        You're right! A poster at a show.
        That's where I saw it. I've been waiting
        A long time for a proper clue.
        I'll check some stores now, thanks to you.

1.40 I'm sure I'll trace it." John smiles shyly,
Picks up his cookie from his plate.
Janet reads out her fortune, wryly:
"*For better luck you have to wait*
Till winter. What's it now, September?
Come speedily, O numb November.
Congeal my fingers. Cigarette?"
"You know I don't. Here's mine: *Forget*
The entanglement of love; forget not
To practice charity. You see—
The cookie says love's not for me."
"John, I've a better dictum: *Set not*
Any great store by cookies; set
Your boat on course and spread your net."

1.41 John kisses Janet swiftly, lightly.
The waiter sets the check by John.
Jan frowns. They pay, and Jan politely
Thanks him and leaves a tip upon
The cookie plate. She thinks, "Why bother?
There's always something or the other,
And even good men of goodwill. . . .
Poor guy. We kept him waiting. Still,
I wish . . . but what's the use? It's trivial,
I guess." When John attempts to hold
The door for her, she thinks, "Why scold
Him for such slips? It's been convivial.
Part with a smile!" They smile and part
In friendship, with a lightened heart.

Two

2.1   That midnight, after strenuous drumming
      And an hour's drive for Liquid Sheep,
      After the catcalls of homecoming,
      Janet's arm hurts. She cannot sleep.
      For hours she stands and views Orion,
      The Bear, the Dog, the Goat, the Lion,
      The cats asleep now, slackly curled
      Upon the surface of the World
      Of Counterpane. Then, suddenly smiling,
      A light within her almond eyes,
      To her grandmother's desk she flies,
      Seized by a notion so beguiling
      That she must—must?—she thinks a bit—
      She must act instantly on it.

2.2   The fitful pen moves on the paper.
It pauses to delete a phrase,
Doodles a face, attempts to caper
Across a dubious word, but stays
Poised in midair. "If injudicious,
At least this won't be meretricious;
But individuality—
How do I strike that note? Let's see,
If I used. . . ." Outside, day is dawning.
Opus complete, and at the sill
She stands in thought. Eight. Nine. But still
The city sleeps. (Ah, Sunday morning,
Most blesséd of all times.) She sets
Her breakfast out, and feeds the pets.

2.3   Sated with requisite nutrition
They eye her milk and Weetabix
As she reads out her composition:
"*Young handsome yuppie, 26,*
Straight, forward, sociable, but lonely,
Cannot believe that he's the only
Well-rounded and well-meaning square
Lusting for love. If you, out there,
Are friendly, female, under 30,
Impulsive, fit, and fun, let's meet.
Be rash. Box——. Cuff, off that sheet!
It's just been typed, and now it's dirty.
I guess your paw prints . . . (The cats purr.)
. . . Can serve in place of signature."

2.4 Brown paper packets, marked discreetly,
From the *Bay Guardian* arrive
Each week: within lie, nested neatly,
A clutch of envelopes. When five
Such packets lie on Janet's table
(Thinner each week) and she is able
To sense a dwindling of the tranche
That seemed at first an avalanche,
She slits the packets to examine
The postmark on each envelope,
Thinking, "I wonder if he'll cope
As sanguinely with glut as famine."
She counts the letters—eighty-two—
And wonders, fiercely, what to do.

2.5 "So many! Jesus! Should I vet them,
Select a few and pass them on,
Or curb myself, abstain, and let them
Wing their uncensored way to John—
Expectant, uncurtailed, each letter
Pleading its own defense? It's better,
Surely, to yield to laissez-faire
And burden him with bulk than dare
Presume to cull his choice by proxy,
Picking my path through torrid lines,
Pert promises and suave designs
From dulcet Deborah to foxy
Farah—a world of tendered joys,
A passion play of pleas and ploys."

2.6   Two mornings after Janet fires
        Her postal charge, she's roused from sleep.
        A chilled voice on the phone inquires:
        "You sent it? Janet, you're a creep.
        You didn't fool me for a minute—
        But would you care to know what's in it?
        It's wasted, I would say, on me—
        My interest in pornography
        Is somewhat jaded. Still, I'm curious:
        Why did you choose to loose this host
        Of bacchantes on me through the post?
        Ought I to thank you?" "You sound furious."
        "Your crazy ad—" she hears him shout,
        "Was garbage in and garbage out!"

2.7   "Come, John, where is your sense of humor?"
        "It's dormant since last night." "But since
        A good man wrote it, I'd assume a
        Few pleasant women might evince
        A favorable—who knows?—inviting
        Response; I'd find it quite exciting.
        How could they all be maenads mad
        With morbid lust? Is it that bad?"
        "Well, while we're on the subject, Janet,
        Since you're charmed by your scheme, and I
        Am a mere blameless passerby,
        I think it's better if you ran it.
        No doubt your modest maidens will
        Quiver to your responsive quill."

2.8 "John, don't get mad. Just think it over."
     "You're too much. Look, I'm late for work.
     I've got to go." "O demon-lover,
     Drive carefully." "I will, O jerk."
     But loosed upon the frenzied freeway,
     He gives no quarter, grace, or leeway
     To lesser cars within the law.
     Tight-lipped, he hears the Peugeot roar
     Past little Bugs and harmless Hondas
     At 90 m.p.h., his mind
     Pulsing with anger, while behind,
     Unnoticed, the deft anacondas
     Of the road-jungle glide in fast:
     The cops catch up with him at last.

2.9 Lights flash. "Oh God! This means a ticket."
     The siren wails. John brakes. "Well, I'm
     Just going to tell them they can stick it...."
     A cop comes. "License, please.... This time
     It's just a fine. The speed you're going
     Is hazardous. How about slowing
     Your pace a little, Mr. Brown?"
     John hears him with a restive frown,
     With more impatience than repentance.
     "Officer, work begins at eight."
     The cop says, "Better late than 'late,' "
     Signing his ticket on that sentence.
     "Have a good day, now!" But John, cross,
     Can't work, and quarrels with his boss.

2.10   A fellow engineer's been fired.
John pleads his cause. ("What's done is done,"
His boss replies.) At evening, tired,
He drives back on Route 101.
Above the rush-hour droves, commuting
Bumper to bumper, horns are hooting.
Through the concussive gas fumes John
Sees *Goodnight, Lemmings!* scrawled upon
An overpass. A stern contralto
Bays Wagner out on "Listener's Choice."
An overripe announcer's voice
States, "KDFC, Pah-lo Ahl-to."
John turns his knob from rival bands
Till KOME's on his hands.

2.11   The freeway sweeps past humming pylons,
Past Canterbury Carpet Mart,
Warehouses, ads displaying nylons
On shapely legs that make John start.
A cigarette ad, sweet and suborning,
Subverts the Surgeon General's warning:
A craggy golfer, tanned, blue-eyed,
Insouciantly stands beside
A Porsche-caged blonde; coolly patrician,
He puffs a menthol-tipped King-size.
John tries to curb his vagrant eyes
And heed the poet's admonition:
"Beneath this slab John Brown is stowed.
He watched the ads and not the road."

2.12　　But in five minutes other features
　　　　Divert him: "Honk for Jesus." "I
　　　　Swerve to run over little creatures."
　　　　"The President is a lesbian spy."
　　　　"Nuke the nukes," "Fan of David Bowie"
　　　　Or "Here today—and gone to Maui,"
　　　　"I ♣ winos," "I ♥ L.A."
　　　　Or "Have you hugged your whale today?"
　　　　"Bartenders do it with more spirit."
　　　　"Old beach boys do it with good vibes."
　　　　John sighs, looks up. An ad describes
　　　　The Roach Motel's compelling merit:
　　　　"Roaches check in—but they don't check out!"
　　　　John thinks, "That's what my life's about."

2.13　　Need John's life be so bug-infested?
　　　　He wasn't always so alone.
　　　　Entrepreneurial, double-breasted,
　　　　He's changed from what his friends have known.
　　　　Work, and the syndrome of possessions
　　　　Leave little time for life's digressions.
　　　　At college, walking down the hall,
　　　　You'd meet your friends. But now it's all
　　　　Too complicated. . . . Scattered, sifted,
　　　　From New York City to L.A.,
　　　　They write, "We must meet up some day . . .";
　　　　Yet even those who haven't drifted
　　　　—Like Phil, or Jan—too far from John,
　　　　He's chary to encroach upon.

2.14   His work's use does not disconcert him;
At least, not much. John feels that what
He chooses to ignore can't hurt him;
Some things are his concern, some not.
His politics have strongly, slowly,
Rigidified; nor does this wholly
Stem from his tenure in Defense.
It's a reflection, in a sense,
Of a rigidity deeper-seated.
A bit of an emotional waif
Since, a small boy, he used to chafe
Against the fate that he'd been meted,
The mother's love he'd never had,
He'd clung to "standards," good or bad.

2.15   Mumbling, as he turns off the freeway,
"Christ, what a day!" he drives his car
Beyond the Bay Bridge piers, the seaway,
The Ferry Building, to a bar,
In search of ... what? Oh, any dumb thing—
Love, company, oblivion—something
To breach this fearsome solitude.
Two bourbons down, in cheerier mood,
He thinks less of the ungiving fetters
Of his bleak life, the Universe,
And how things must get worse and worse,
Than of the intriguing cache of letters,
Almost untouched, back in his flat.
"I'll read a few. No harm in that!"

2.16   Back home, he spreads them in his study,
Boosts his intention with, "Godspeed!
You've got to get your fingers muddy
When panning gold," and starts to read.
The first one, waxing weird and wayward,
Comes from a doomed housewife in Hayward;
The next, from Kate in mad Marin,
Is redolent of Chanel and gin;
The third ... but why describe the riot
Of paper, color, scent, device,
Construction, style? Let it suffice
That, dazed by this immoderate diet
("Too much confectionery, too rich"),
John can't remember which is which.

2.17   Yes, why describe the louche lubricious
Dreams of a Daly City Dame,
The half-enticing, subtly vicious
Burblings of Belle from Burlingame,
And then from Eve of San Francisco,
"Six novel ways of using Crisco,"
Or the Tigress of Tiburon
Who waits to pounce on hapless John.
Still, trapped in this traumatic traffic,
Silly and frilly, cool and hot,
John finds about a quarter not
Too evidently pornographic.
Of these he gingerly picks three.
"The others just aren't right for me."

2.18   Selection made, John now dispatches
Three crisp and courtly notes, and waits
Unhurriedly. The act detaches
His heart from gloom, leaves to the Fates
What lies within their proper region.
To each of the residual legion
He sends in a plain envelope
The photocopied lines: *I hope*
You will excuse this xeroxed letter.
I do not think that you and I
Are matched, but thanks for your reply
To my ad, and I wish you better
Luck for the future. John. He signs,
But adds no surname to the lines.

2.19   In his notes, though, he begs the pleasure
On three successive Saturdays
(If they should chance to have the leisure)
Of the three women at three plays
Followed by dinner. Wasp Bluestocking
Accepts, and turns up with a shocking
Pink parasol. They see *Macbeth*,
Where John's bored to an inch of death
By her insistent exegesis:
Appearance and reality themes
And the significance of dreams
And darkness, and the singular thesis
That the Third Murderer is in fact
The central figure of each act.

2.20   Throughout the play she oozes jargon.
Throughout the meal she oozes French
Till John is numbed inert as argon.
He grows quite pale. "Aroint thee, wench!"
He thinks, but keeps a fragile patter
Feebly afloat. "Why, what's the matter?
You look as white as Banquo's ghost
Force-fed three slices of milk toast."
She laughs genteelly at her sally.
"Just indigestion," John replies.
When the time comes to leave, he sighs,
"Lately, my work in Silicon Valley
Leaves no time for *affaires de coeur*,"
And bids a glad adieu to her.

2.21   Belinda Beale's acceptance letter
Arrives (with photograph). John smiles.
"Surely Belinda will be better:
What eyes!" Unconscious of her wiles
John waits; exactly one week later
He goes with her to the theater
To see that interesting play
Cat on a Hot Tin Roof. Halfway
Through the third act, her dexterous digits,
With small attempt at camouflage,
Engage in passionate pétrissage*
Along his thigh. John squirms and fidgets.
He darts her a swift glance. She stops,
But not for long. The curtain drops.

pétrissage: "massage by longitudinal rubbing and lateral
squeezing" (*The Chambers Dictionary*)

2.22   At dinner amorous Belinda
        Stares deep, deep, with her peerless eyes
        And tries to spark John's dampened tinder
        With coos and flutings. "Ah," she sighs,
        "You're such a fox!" John frowns and flushes.
        Immune to his beleaguered blushes,
        With "Oh, your accent is so cute!"
        She strikes her helpless victim mute,
        While underneath the elegant table
        Of coq au vin, to John's disgust,
        Discomfiture, and rising lust,
        She . . . John gets up, concocts a fable,
        "Ten-thirty!—got to go—my wife—"
        Leaves fifty bucks, and flees for life.

2.23   "Too bad," he thinks. "Well, third time lucky."
        He waits for A.T.F.'s response.
        "I liked her letter; she sounds plucky
        And amicable. For the nonce
        I think that's what I need. Belinda
        Would have combusted me to cinder
        And Wasp stung me to learnéd death."
        Her letter comes. With indrawn breath
        John reads the note, the friendly greeting,
        The lines (as usual, typed). They say:
        Since my job's taking me away
        From San Francisco soon, our meeting
        Would serve no aim. Forgive me, please;
        I've just been told this. Anne T. Friese.

35

2.24   "The King's third daughter," John thinks sadly.
"If this were just a fairy tale. . . .
Why am I taking this so badly?
She's just a name brought by the mail,
Gone with the wind." To her box number
He writes: *Anne, I don't mean to lumber*
Once more into your consciousness,
But if you left me your address
We could maintain communication.
This is returned: *Box Number Changed.*
Thus Janet (alias Anne)'s arranged
Her creature's discontinuation.
She feels the note she wrote for fun
Would have been better unbegun.

2.25   At breakfast, sipping a Bacardi
And Coke, Jan meditates upon
Her guilt. She forwards seven tardy
Responses to the ad to John.
John reads these with faint aspiration.
Each seems a standard variation
On themes he's heard too loud and long.
"The Rhine maidens have sung their song;
This straggling coda is bathetic . . .
(He reads the fifth one) . . . It's a farce . . .
(The sixth one) . . . And it came to pass
That John stayed celibate and ascetic.
Good! Curtain down, and weak applause."
The seventh letter gives him pause.

2.26   He reads it through twice, somewhat chary
Of yet one more time being had.
It goes: *Dear Yuppie, I am wary*
Of answering a personal ad.
This is the first time, I should mention,
That I have broken my convention
Of reticence. But, well, here goes:
I rather liked your literate prose.
As an attorney, the clear crafting
Of words (our stock-in-trade) excites
My admiration. Nothing blights
A document like sloppy drafting.
Your ad, if I may be allowed
To matronize you, does you proud.

2.27   *I'm friendly, female, 27,*
Well-rounded too, and somewhat square.
I've not yet known romantic heaven,
But harbor hopes of getting there.
I'm fit—at least, I'm not convulsive;
And fun, I hope, though not impulsive.
To match the handsomeness you flaunt
(I do not mean this as a taunt;
I find immodesty disarming),
I have heard several people say
I am good-looking, in my way.
So if you'd like to meet, Prince Charming,
That shows discernment. If you flout
My charms, you are a tasteless lout.

2.28   *With all good wishes. Yours sincerely,*
              Elisabeth Dorati (Liz).
              John reads, but sees no image clearly.
              At times it seems as if she is
              Nervous and stern, at others hearty.
              Who is Elisabeth Dorati:
              A cool manipulating minx
              Or a wise imperturbable sphinx?
              The hand's italic, warm and vigorous,
              Crossed out, at times, with a clean line.
              The paper's cream, of plain design
              (No scent or frill), the ink's a rigorous
              Black, and the pen, though narrow-tipped,
              Maintains the strength of the clear script.

2.29   How could John know that Liz Dorati
              (Ex-Stanford Law School, last year's batch)
              Is neither cool nor stern nor hearty,
              And much sought after as a match
              By more than one well-heeled attorney
              At the staid law firm Cobb & Kearny?
              Daily their sheepish, prurient eyes
              Swerve from their statutes to her thighs.
              Unmoved by this redundant bounty,
              Liz spends her weekends at her folks':
              A vineyard where she reads and soaks
              The sunlight of Sonoma County,
              Talks to her dad of must and vines,
              Plays chess with him, and sips his wines.

2.30   Though Liz was brought up marinading
       Near the jacuzzis of Marin,
       She never reveled in parading
       Her heart, her knowledge, or her skin.
       She bloomed unhardened by her beauty,
       Immune to "Lizzie, you're a cutie!"
       Though doting aunt and bleating beau
       Reiterated it was so.
       Her mother, anxious, loving, rigid,
       Said, "Liz, a pretty girl like you
       Ought to be thinking of..." "Et tu?"
       Sighed Liz, "Mom, do you think I'm frigid?
       Just let me get my law degree
       Out of the way—and then, I'll see."

2.31   Though while at law school Liz had wandered
       Into the odd affair or two,
       So far at least she had not squandered
       Her time or heart on someone who
       Appeared a candidate for marriage.
       Mrs. Dorati might disparage
       Her children (Liz and Ed and Sue)
       For proving such a fruitless crew;
       Yet all her gentle instigation
       ("When I was your age, Ed ... don't frown ...
       You really ought to settle down....")
       Had foundered in the generation
       Of the desired posse of
       Grandchildren she could spoil and love.

2.32   Liz seemed immersed in her career
        (For which Miss Simms of fifth-grade math
        Must bear the blame—who made Liz veer
        Toward a more professional path
        Than had been planned by Liz's mother).
        Ed too had no "significant other"
        (Or none, at least, who could be seen).
        And Sue in recent years had been
        So captivated by the cello
        That bows and rosin and Mozart,
        Not beaus and roses, filled her heart.
        Although life's autumn, sere and yellow,
        Now pattered round their mother's days,
        The kids preserved their childless ways.

2.33   Yet Liz, sweet Liz, a little lonely,
        Sequestered in her city flat
        (Unlike her student days), with only
        The trusty Charlemagne, her cat,
        A fearsome tabby, as companion—
        Felt, as she swam the rapid canyon
        Of her career, while crocodiles
        Nibbled her toes with savory smiles,
        That there must be some happy medium
        Between a legal partner's life
        And being a legal partner's wife.
        O loneliness—or else, O tedium!
        And so one day she hit upon
        The personal ads and, through them, John.

2.34   In fact her letter cost Liz dearly.
       Skimming the paper, flipping through
       Its pungent *cris de coeur*, she nearly
       Passed John's ad by. The word that drew
       Her gaze was "square." She'd often pondered
       Her own geometry, and wondered
       About a possible congruence.
       Could this be it? A second sense
       Nudged second thoughts aside. Though cringing
       At her unprecedented act,
       With a brash pen and muzzled tact,
       A quickening heartbeat and a singeing
       Blush, she composed and swiftly wrote,
       Signed, sealed, addressed, and sent her note.

2.35   On Sunday morning, groomed and waiting,
       John sits in the Café Trieste.
       A canny veteran of blind dating
       (Twice bitten, once shy), it is best
       To meet, he reckons, far from drama,
       In daylight: less romantic, calmer,
       And, if things should not turn out right,
       Convenient for ready flight.
       At noon, the meeting hour appointed,
       A tall, fresh-faced blonde enters, sees
       The suited John. "Excuse me, please . . .
       (A little hesitant and disjointed)
       . . . Would you be—John?" John smiles. "Correct.
       And you're Elisabeth, I suspect."

2.36   "She's lovely," John thinks, almost staring.
They shake hands. John's heart gives a lurch.
"Handsome, all right, and what he's wearing
Suggests he's just returned from church. . . .
Sound, solid, practical, and active,"
Thinks Liz, "I find him quite attractive.
Perhaps. . . ." All this has been inferred
Before the first substantive word
Has passed between the two. John orders
A croissant and espresso; she
A sponge cake and a cup of tea.
They sit, but do not breach the borders
Of discourse till, at the same time,
They each break silence with, 'Well, I'm—"

2.37   Both stop, confused. Both start together:
"I'm sorry—" Each again stops dead.
They laugh. "It hardly matters whether
You speak or I," says John: "I said,
Or meant to say—I'm glad we're meeting."
Liz quietly smiles, without completing
What she began. "Not fair," says John.
"Come clean. What was it now? Come on:
One confidence deserves another."
"No need," says Liz. "You've said what I
Would have admitted in reply."
They look, half smiling, at each other,
Half puzzled too, as if to say,
"I don't know why I feel this way."

2.38   Around them arias from Rossini
        Resound from wall to wall. A bum
        Unsoberly demands Puccini.
        Cups clink. Aficionados hum
        And sing along with Pavarotti,
        Expatiate upon the knotty
        Dilemmas of the world, peruse
        The *Examiner* for sports or news
        Or, best of all, the funny pages,
        Where Garfield, that egregious cat,
        Grows daily lazier and more fat,
        And voluble polemic rages,
        While praise by one and all's expressed
        For the black brew of the Trieste.

2.39   The pair are now rapt in discussion.
        Jan comes in, sees them, cannot hear
        What they are saying—could be Russian
        For all she knows; she does not steer
        Too close, takes in the situation,
        Sees John's face boyish with elation,
        While Liz (Who's she?) with vibrant verve
        In an exhilarating curve
        Of explication or description
        Looks radiant. Jan reflects, "Somehow
        I feel ... Oh Christ! ... I feel, right now,
        I don't want coffee. My Egyptian
        Deities wait at home for food.
        I'll come back when I'm in the mood."

2.40   Unnoticed, Janet leaves, abstracted
By her abortive coffee break.
Back in the café, Liz, attracted
By John's absorption, nibbles cake,
Sips tea, doffs her defensive armor
And, laughing, thinks, "This man's a charmer.
I like him, and he likes me, though
I can't imagine why it's so."
(O nightingales! O moon! O roses!)
In talk as heady as champagne
She mentions her cat, Charlemagne:
"A wondrous cat!" John laughs, proposes
A toast: "The King and Queen of France
And England. Far may they advance.

2.41   Well may they reign. Long may they flourish."
Happy (with just a dash of pain),
He drains his cup. "But now to nourish
My hopes of meeting you again—
What do you say—next Thursday—seven—
For dinner at the Tree of Heaven—
Say that you'll come—it's in the Haight—
A movie afterwards at eight?"
Liz thinks, "There's my gestalt group meeting.
I didn't go last week. I should
(The leader said) come if I could
This Thursday...." But the thought is fleeting.
She says, "Thanks, John," and the pair parts
By shaking hands (with shaking hearts).

2.42   The days pass in a picosecond—
       The days pass slowly, each a year—
       Depending on how time is reckoned.
       Liz, floating in the stratosphere
       Of daydreams, sees the hours go flying.
       For John they linger, amplifying
       The interval until they meet.
       The sun seems almost to retreat.
       At last it's Thursday. John, ecstatic,
       Arrives first, stares at the decor
       (Arboreal), then at the door . . .
       And Liz's entrance is dramatic:
       A deep blue dress to emphasize
       The sapphire spirit of her eyes.

2.43   Her gold hair's fashioned, not severely,
       Into a bun. From a gold chain
       A single pearl, suspended clearly,
       Allures his eye. John, once again,
       Can't speak for wonder and confusion:
       A woman, or divine illusion?
       He overcomes his vertigo
       And stands. He mutters, "Liz, hello.
       I hope . . . was it a hassle finding
       This place?" His voice fails. He sits down.
       Liz says, "You're nervous, Mr. Brown.
       Don't worry; I too need reminding
       That this is real." In an unplanned
       Gesture of warmth, she takes his hand.

2.44   John looks downwards, as if admonished,
Then slowly lifts his head, and sighs.
Half fearfully and half astonished
They look into each other's eyes.
The waiter, bearded, burly, macho,
Says, "Madam, though it's cold, gazpacho
Is what I'd recommend. Noisettes
Of lamb, perhaps, or mignonettes
Of veal to follow. . . ." Unavailing
Are his suggestions. Nothing sinks
Into their ears. "Ah, well," he thinks,
"They're moonstruck. It'll be plain sailing.
Lovers, despite delays and slips
And rotten service, leave large tips."

2.45   Liz, floundering in a confusion
Of spirit, starts to speak: "Today
We fought a case about collusion. . . ."
John says, "I don't know what to say.
Liz, since we met, I think I'm losing
My mind—O God, it's so confusing—
I thought it was a joke, but when
We met, I realized—and then
Today, once more—it seems I'm flailing
Around for something—and I feel
An ache too desperate for repeal
Or cure—as if my heart were failing.
I was transported Sunday. Then
You left; the pain began again."

2.46   His voice is lowered, lost, appealing,
Rinsed of all wit, of all pretense.
Liz, helpless in a surge of feeling,
An undertow to common sense,
Finds that she has assumed the tender
Reincarnation of dream vendor.
Her eyes mist over with a glaze
Of sympathy. She gently says,
"Why do you find it so surprising
That you are happy? Are you sad
So often—tell me, John. I'm glad
That we've indulged in advertising,
But—having met you—it would seem
You feel all life's a shaky dream."

2.47   As in an airless room a curtain
Parts to admit the evening breeze,
So John's exhausted and uncertain
Tension admits a transient ease,
And Liz's lenient mediation
Smooths out his doubt and hesitation.
She looks at him: "Don't be afraid
I'll find what you say bland or staid."
Relieved of the unspoken duty
Of cleverness and coolness now
John brings himself to speak, somehow,
Of truth, ambition, status, beauty,
The hopes (or dupes) for which we strive,
The ghosts that keep the world alive.

2.48   But talk turns, as the meal progresses,
To (heart-unsettling) movie stars,
The chef's (mouth-watering) successes,
The ills (mind-boggling) of their cars,
To cats, to microchips, flotation
Of corporate bonds, sunsets, inflation,
Their childhoods ... while, along the way,
A bountiful, rich cabernet
Bestows its warm, full-bodied flavor
On everything they touch upon,
But most of all on Liz and John
Who, fluent as the draught they savor,
In phrase both fulsome and condign
Sing praise of Californian wine.

2.49   Cut to dessert. An apt potation
Of amaretto. They forgo
The cinema for conversation,
And hand in hand they stroll below
The fog-transfigured Sutro Tower,
A masted galleon at this hour,
Adjourn for ice cream, rich and whole,
At Tivoli's, near Carl and Cole;
Next for a drive—refreshing drama
Of changing streets and changeless bay
And, where the fog has cleared away,
The exquisite bright panorama
Of streetlights, sea-lights, starlight spread
Above, below, and overhead.

2.50   The night is cold. It's late November.
They stand close, shivering side by side,
Chilled by the ice cream, yet an ember,
A flare, ignited by the ride,
This staring at the lights together,
Defends them from inclement weather.
They stand, half shivering, half still,
Below the tower on Telegraph Hill,
Not speaking, with a finger tracing
The unseen lines from star to star.
Liz turns. They kiss. They kiss, they are
Caught in a panic of embracing.
They cannot hold each other tight
Enough against the chill of night.

2.51   Daybreak. John wakes to sunlight streaming
Across an unfamiliar bed.
"A cream duvet? I must be dreaming—
With lilac hexagons—instead
Of my plain blanket—and the ceiling:
An open glass skylight revealing
Clear sky—and what's this on my feet?
A cat! My God!—" With swift heartbeat
He starts as, through the door he's facing,
Liz enters with a coffee tray
In negligible negligee.
She pours two cups. Without embracing
They sit, their eyes infused with sleep
And love, and drink the potion deep.

2.52   It's Friday, though; the office beckons.
        (No time for sleep or love, no time
        To shave now.) John's boss frowns; he reckons
        There's been a hitch: "Oh, hi, John—I'm
        A bit concerned about this bubble
        Memory. . . ." John strokes his stubble
        And hums as beatifically
        As a sun-sated bumblebee
        Besotted by the soft vibration
        Of his own pollen-dusted wings,
        Oblivious to other things
        Than his congenial meditation.
        He says, "What bubble memory?"
        His boss gawks at him pityingly.

2.53   But Liz, with promptitude and pertness,
        Displaying a resplendent smile,
        A near-extravagant alertness,
        And murmuring, "When in doubt, file,"
        Storms through (in spite of all distractions)
        A block of six Secure Transactions
        In record time. Her colleagues sigh:
        "Poor Liz—I'm sure she must be high."
        (One mutters: "Coke—she looks so hyper."
        Another: "Acid can be rough.
        I wonder where she gets the stuff."
        A third: "Speed leads to speed." With riper
        Worldliness, her boss says: "She's
        Hooked on a stronger drug than these.")

2.54 John's watch beeps out the hour of seven.
   Liz meets him, but this time outside
   A theater near the Tree of Heaven
   To see the movie they denied
   Themselves last night. They choose to tender
   Ill-judged obeisance to Fassbinder.
   Ten minutes of *Veronika Voss*
   And John says, "Liz, I'm at a loss.
   What's this about?" "Beats me!" "Your attic
   Or my flat?" "Either! Mine?" "Let's go."
   Through the skylight the Pleiads glow
   And soon, despite the operatic
   Dissonances of Charlemagne,
   The loving pair make love again.

2.55 The loving pair has bit the apple
   Of mortal knowledge. As we see
   The rosy half-light of love's chapel
   Halo their ardent heads, should we
   Hymn them in accents hushed and holy?
   Forbear, O Gentle Reader. Slowly,
   Ah, slowly, from their whim-swept height
   Of rash delirium and delight
   All sober inklings of perspective
   Sink in the Wash of tenderness. . . .
   Far better, since my life's a mess,
   To spray the mooncalfs with invective.
   Why do they look so pleased, when I
   Am loverless and pine, and sigh?

2.56   Who was it said, "Love is the friction
Of two skins"? From "Your place or mine?"
There follow weeks of sweet addiction
To insular if sparkling wine.
Liz, now addressed by John as "honey,"
Responds to him with "funny bunny."
Their diction has, alas, become
Incomprehensible and numb.
Their brains appear to be dissolving
To sugary sludge as they caress.
In lieu of fire, force, finesse,
We have a ballet now involving
A pretty pas de deux instead,
With common Walkmans on their head.

2.57   Judged by these artless serfs of Cupid,
Love is not blind but, rather, dumb.
Their babblings daily grow more stupid.
I am embarrassed for them. Come,
Let's leave them here, the blessèd yuppies,
As happy as a pair of puppies,
Or doves, who with their croodlings might
Make even Cuff and Link seem bright.
Let's leave them to their fragile fictions—
Arcadia, Shangri-la, Cockaigne—
A land beyond the reach of pain—
Except for two slight contradictions,
To wit ... but what transpires next
Is furnished later in this text.

Three

3.1   As Liz and John move out of focus
      Into an amorous mist, let's shift
      Our lens, Dear Reader, to a locus
      An hour south along that rift
      That unnerves half of California:
      Not just the crusty cohorts born here
      But all who earn their bread and salt
      Along the San Andreas Fault.
      Commerce and learning, manufacture
      And government proceed above,
      And nature's loveliness, and love;
      Beneath them lies the hideous fracture,
      Author of the convulsive shocks
      That rip the hills and split the rocks.

3.2 A tow-haired boy sits with his father
Upon a rock that caps a hill.
The son (Paul) says that he would rather
Catch centipedes. The father (Phil,
John's school chum, whom we mentioned earlier)
Looks on amused as Paul grows surlier.
Paul's six, his father's twenty-eight;
And as they sit and altercate,
Phil rests his hand on his son's shoulder.
"When I was his age," Phil recalls,
"My moods were as unfixed as Paul's.
I wonder why, as we grow older..."
Paul cuts in: "Dad, you're going bald."
"I know," replies Phil, unenthralled.

3.3 Phil meditates on his condition:
"They say that our maternal genes
Determine our predisposition
To lose hair.... If that's true, that means...
(Crumbling a dry oak leaf, he scratches
His head, and fingers his bald patches
Exploratively, rubs his nose,
And takes his glasses off.)... Suppose...
(His brows crease up in meditation)
... Instead of losing hair, it were
To coat our forehead like a fur
And then usurp, in swift migration,
Our eyes, cheeks, lips.... I guess, all told,
It's good that we grow bald when old."

3.4 Soothed by such counterfactual reason
   Phil's thoughts turn from his homely face
   To the crisp features of the season:
   The straw-gold hill, this oak-strewn place,
   With here the flutter of a dusty
   Sparrow, and there the encroaching rusty
   Lichen upon the rock where Paul
   Sits singing to himself, and all
   The hillsides burred with skeletal thistles
   And thornbush, and the clear cool air
   Presaging winter rain, and there
   A mockingbird with chacks and whistles
   Liquidly aviating through
   A sky of Californian blue.

3.5 Two brittle oaks in dark rigidity,
   Bare-branched and canted, crown the crest.
   Above the rock with swift fluidity
   A scrub jay flashes to its nest
   —A cyan flicker—where the greenery
   Of mistletoe revives the scenery
   Entangled in the generous boughs
   Of its old host; and cattle browse
   Along the moister gullies, scattering
   As joggers, pulsing with intent,
   Strive ridge-wards, hell- or heaven-bent,
   Stern-visaged, gasping, frothing, battering
   The patient earth with the curt beat
   Of itchy soles and athletes' feet.

3.6   The distant cattle's baleful lowing,
The distance runners' stoic pace,
The way the distant world is going
Crazy—the space and missile race—
The job Phil left in Datatronics
(Hive of robotics and moronics)
Preoccupy him as he smokes
At ease beneath the tilting oaks.
While firms were wooing him and clamoring
To lease from him his soul and brains,
Phil shocked his friends and slipped his chains.
The SOS his heart was hammering
Had grown too loud to be ignored....
Thus Phil reflects; his son is bored.

3.7   Paul now petitions for a story.
"What? Oh, OK. Let's see ... (Phil blinks.)
... This one is called *Chromiska's Glory*.
About a cat ... (He pauses, thinks.)
... There was a cat who, when a kitten,
Liked drinking ink, and had been bitten
By several rats...." "How large?" "This big."
"Oh! ... Go on, Dad." Phil snaps a twig.
He rubs his nose in concentration.
"Now as a kitten she had lapped
Up so much ink...." Paul listens, rapt.
His father warms to his narration.
Paul cups his chin, the plot swings free,
And twenty minutes pass like three.

3.8　"...And that is why the cat Chromiska
　　　Grew silver-haired that winter night
　　　Down to her last eyelash and whisker.
　　　When people asked, was it from fright,
　　　Her friends said no, but would not tell them
　　　About the snowstorm that befell them—
　　　And to this day, the reason's known
　　　To you, me, and the cats alone."
　　　Phil sips a Michelob, and, serious,
　　　Looks at his son, whose deep brown eyes
　　　Return his gaze with pleased surprise.
　　　Paul says, "Chromiska!" Then, imperious:
　　　"Tell me another, Dad." Phil starts
　　　The Story of Three Apple Tarts.

3.9　"Once, in a country green and hilly
　　　There lived three bakers. One was fat
　　　And friendly, one was slim and silly,
　　　And one had whiskers like a cat.
　　　You should have smelt their warm bread baking,
　　　But, best of all, when they were making
　　　Fresh apple tarts, that's when the scent
　　　Rose to a grateful firmament. . . ."
　　　"What's 'firmament'?" Phil, somewhat chastened,
　　　Says, "Sky. Where was I? Well, up there,
　　　There was a great and greedy Bear
　　　—I'll point him out tonight—who hastened
　　　To find out where this glorious scent
　　　Was coming from. So down he went.

3.10   He heard the silly baker humming
A song called 'Apple of My Heart,'
While the bewhiskered one was drumming
And yelling, 'Sweet as apple tart!'—
And the fat baker roared with laughter
And shouted, 'Appily ever after.'
The hungry Bear now grew afraid.
He smelled the fresh-baked tarts, all laid
Deliciously upon the table.
He stood and trembled near the door
Till he could stand the smell no more.
He thought, 'If only I were able
To steal one tart—one tart, that's all.
I'll leave them two. I promise.' . . . Paul!"

3.11   For Paul has upped and gone exploring
And now is nowhere to be found.
Phil wonders, "Was my epic boring?
Where's he gone off to? . . ." On the ground,
Stretched out, examining a spider,
Paul sprawls, his mouth expanding wider
As, suddenly, he sees it rise.
Phil walks up to him where he lies
And puts his hand upon his shoulder.
His son says, "Wow, Dad, did you see?
It went straight up into the tree."
Phil answers, "Son, it's getting colder.
Put on your coat." Paul says, "Dad, get
A spider for us as a pet."

3.12   "No." "Why not?" "Spiders have weird habits."
        "I like them." "I don't." "I do." "Let's
        Get something we both like, like rabbits."
        "Why rabbits, Dad?" "They make great pets.
        Your mother used to like...." Phil falters,
        Halts in mid-utterance and alters
        What he had meant to say. "Well, son—
        You want a spider? We'll get one.
        Put on your coat now...." As they linger,
        Paul sees a green patch on the plain.
        "A field?" "A lake, when filled with rain."
        "And that?" Paul points a questioning finger
        At Stanford's roofs of clay-baked red.
        "A school." ... "You talk like Mom is dead."

3.13   An abrupt torque of pain and sorrow
        Wrenches Phil's heart. He stares at Paul.
        (Claire's haunted eyes.) "First thing tomorrow
        We'll get that spider for you." All
        Diversion is in vain. Though quiet,
        Paul's heart beats with a sudden riot
        Of lonely fear. At first he keeps
        Himself in check, but then he weeps,
        Turns from his father, half accusing;
        Without a word, he sobs and cries
        And folds his arms across his eyes
        And sits and hugs himself, refusing
        Solace or love or father's hand,
        Lost in his forfeit motherland.

3.14   Phil puts his arms around him, kisses
       His grimy face and says, "Don't cry...."
       "Poor boy," he thinks, "I guess he misses
       His mother even more than I.
       It's been a year, Claire, since your leaving.
       If you just knew how he's been grieving—
       Or what it's like to be alone
       When you are six. Couldn't you phone
       Or write just a few lines, or visit
       Him sometimes—at the very least
       Send him some small gift from back East?
       Are you too busy? Poor? What is it?
       Why can't you write? Why don't you? Why?
       You love your son as much as I.

3.15   A year. A year. That snooty tweedy
       Son-of-an-East-Coast-bitch—I thought
       You'd see right through his act, his weedy
       Compliant charm—or would have fought
       The flattery, pressure—what?—temptation?
       —What a laugh!—whimsy, inspiration—
       O God, I wish I'd never seen
       Your face—I wish I'd never been
       Married—Claire, Claire, we loved each other.
       We lived together for six years.
       I've shed too many tedious tears
       To cry again. Paul had a mother
       Who kissed him, read to him in bed,
       But he's right, she's as good as dead.

3.16   You said I tried to dominate you.
       What gave you that idea—Claire—
       Why would I want to?—Do I hate you?—
       I think of you and I despair
       Of any happiness without you.
       What wretched loveliness about you
       Makes me still long to see you when
       You've done to me what to most men
       Would have … What's changed? What could
          have changed you?
       You must have loved me to resist
       Your family's unsubtle twist
       When they insisted I'd deranged you—
       Claire Cabot marrying Philip Weiss—
       For all their Wasp stings of advice.

3.17   And living happily ever after—
       Amen—as a good atheist Jew
       Should say. Christ, I can hear their laughter:
       'Poor Claire, we thought he wouldn't do.'
       'Marry in haste, repent at leisure.'
       At least your great-aunts got some pleasure
       Out of the wreck. Perhaps it's true
       They knew you better than you knew
       Yourself—when you were sweet and twenty
       And I was dumb and twenty-one. . . .
       But we were happy, had a son,
       Invested in a piano, plenty
       Of furniture, a Ford Capri,
       Insurance, dishwasher, TV . . .

3.18   ... The works. Sometimes we'd light a fire,
          I at the keyboard, and you'd sing—
          Like the old days in the Bach choir
          Where we first met. Remembering
          Those evenings with the darkness coming,
          Your voice, the whispering flames, my humming—
          While, like an unequal metronome,
          Paul thumped the floor—I think our home
          Was what I'd always longed and prayed for.
          What crept into our happiness?
          What made you leave me, Claire? I guess
          Disfiguring is what dreams are made for.
          A fool in bliss, what made me feel
          Our rings were not soft gold but steel?"

3.19   Such thoughts melt through the frozen river
          Of his sad mind, and yet out loud,
          Seeing Paul quietly weep and shiver,
          He says, taut-featured, head half bowed,
          "No, Paul, she's gone away." "Forever?"
          "I just can't tell you, son—but never
          Think you're alone. You've got me." "When
          Will *you* leave me?" Phil, shocked, stares, then
          Holds Paul (still snot-nosed) to him tightly,
          And says, "Don't say that. You are all
          And everything I care for, Paul.
          I'll never leave you." Then, more brightly,
          "In fact, you know, you'll be the one,
          When you've grown up, to leave me, son.

3.20   Now, let's go home.... It's getting chilly,
       And we've got dinner to prepare."
       Paul gets a free ride down the hilly
       Track to the road, and once down there
       Reluctantly climbs off Phil's shoulder
       Into the small Volkswagen: older,
       Less fancy than the Ford Capri,
       But now, with two instead of three,
       And (since the break with Datatronics)
       No money coming, as Phil says,
       The right car for these straitened days:
       Secondhand, squat, no supersonics
       ("Zero to ninety in seconds flat"),
       But tough and friendly for all that.

3.21   Zucchini from the kitchen garden,
       Potatoes, turkey, kiwi fruit,
       Jell-O that won't consent to harden,
       And cups of chocolate constitute
       The evening meal. Queen of their haven,
       The merry widow Mrs. Craven
       —Plump, sage, and sixty-two—drops by
       With a postprandial pumpkin pie.
       "Now eat this—I don't want to store it."
       "Ah, Mrs. Craven, you're a star!"
       "Baloney! Both you youngsters are
       Starving to death. I can't ignore it."
       With this their landlady carves three
       Great wedges out with gourmet glee.

3.22   "A little brandy, Mrs. Craven?"
        "Well, thank you. . . . Phil, you must take care
        Of your good looks. You're all unshaven.
        Your shirt's unpressed. Look at your hair."
        Phil grumbles, "Mrs. Craven, baking
        Pies to expand my girth, and making
        Fun of my looks—that's really low!"
        "My daughter swears you're handsome." "Oh!"
        Rowena Craven, racy redhead,
        Who blares her stereophonic way
        To craft fairs all around the bay,
        Peddling her quilts, committed Dead-head
        Who totes her bootlegged tapes about,
        Thinks Philip Weiss is just far out.

3.23   Herself embroiled in the peace movement
        (She's taking Russian in night school
        Three times a week "for world improvement"),
        Rowena thinks Phil's ultra-cool
        To leave his job for the sole reason,
        "To go on would have been high treason
        To common sense and humankind."
        Last Thursday evening, when she dined
        In Palo Alto with her mother,
        She mentioned her new flame. "Oh dear!
        Who's the poor man?" "He lives near here."
        "How near?" "Next door." "Oh, choose some other
        Quarry, Rowena. Please don't crush
        Poor Phil's heart into quivering mush."

3.24   Now Paul yawns as he nibbles candy,
        And the pie's vanished, bite by bite,
        And Mrs. Craven's drunk her brandy,
        And the time's come to say good night.
        Now they're alone, and Paul, though sleepy,
        Insists Phil read him "something creepy"
        Out of the grisly Brothers Grimm.
        Phil smooths his pillow, reads to him.
        The boy ingests the gruesome diet
        With equanimity, but soon
        His eyes close. Now Phil hums a tune
        In a voice low, unedged, and quiet
        Until he sees that sleep has come:
        A tune from Brahms Claire used to hum.

3.25   To adjust a portrait too one-sided,
        I ought to state that *in re* Claire
        Informed opinion is divided.
        Her family frowned at Phil's crude air,
        Then shrugged, and tried to absorb their burly,
        Rogue son-in-law who, curt and surly,
        Splattered (to Claire's grief) needless yolk
        Upon her nest of gentlefolk.
        Phil's scorn of "country-clubbing rabble,"
        His jangling views, his uncouth jokes,
        And (once, at Christmas with Claire's folks)
        His use of "queynte" to win at Scrabble,
        Resulted in a virtual ban
        On Phil from the whole Cabot clan.

3.26   Post-marriage incompatibility
       Of taste and style and interest,
       Now hammering on love's fragility,
       Exposed its contract to the test.
       Phil's vigor, once his great attraction,
       Exhausted Claire now; her reaction
       To argument was to withdraw
       Into her life and close the door.
       Fiercely from Florida, Phil's mother,
       Old Mrs. Weiss, defended Claire,
       Declaring with a Delphic air
       That Phil would never find another
       Woman like her, and was to blame
       For Claire's defection when it came.

3.27   To shelter Paul from the anxiety
       Erratic visits might create,
       Claire remained absent. The propriety
       Of this is open to debate,
       But not the tilt of her intention:
       Her pain and loss and apprehension
       At separation from her son
       Grieved her as much as anyone.
       Bewildered by this harsh estrangement,
       Phil closed the piano, sold Claire's pets,
       Paid off the bulk of their joint debts
       And, following the rearrangement
       Of his curbed state, as an unplanned
       Office of love, took Paul in hand.

3.28   It happens that, a few months later,
A concert of three string quartets
Draws Liz back to her alma mater.
She phones John, "I've got tickets; let's
Go down to Stanford. Sue'll be playing.
Ed won't be there, despite my saying
That sibling solidarity
Concerns him just as much as me.
I hope Sue isn't disappointed. . . ."
"The program?" "Mozart, Schönberg, Brahms."
"Ah well, that certainly has charms—
Though you know, darling, how disjointed
These jumbled periods make me feel.
Where are they playing?" "Dinkelspiel."

3.29   "Schönberg's an ulcer-generator."
"Oh, don't be stodgy, John." "OK,
It's a date, honey." Two days later
They hear the Ionian Quartet play:
Four students. Sue draws dark and mellow
Lyrical magic from her cello
In Mozart's last quartet in D.
O loveliness, constrained and free!
Ah, Mozart, prince of music makers
Who (for the miracle you gave)
Lie buried in an unmarked grave!
Now the world movers and world shakers
—Archbishops, stewards, counts, and kings—
Rot voiceless, you still lend us wings.

3.30   Rich, bright, enrapturing, enthralling
Tapestry! As Liz hears them play,
Tears come into her eyes, recalling
That half-forgotten childhood day
When, at the insistence of their mother,
She and her sister and her brother
Were press-ganged into lessons. Ed
Soon dumped his violin, instead
Sustaining through his adolescence
(But turns) guitar, trombone, and sax.
Liz's viola bow grew lax.
But a melodious iridescence
Of joy today envelops Sue
In her Mozartian debut.

3.31   "What a magnificent requital
For all Mom's pains. Too bad she's ill.
It's two hours' drive to the recital
Down from our place; Dad's not young. Still,
Sue said she'd tape the Mozart for them.
Oh well, I'm sure Schönberg would bore them...."
John jams her thought waves to complain,
"This sandwiched Schönberg is a pain...."
Then, in a tone more sour and surly,
"... If only they would condescend
To shift this crap to either end,
We could arrive late or leave early.
Thank God I've brought my earplugs—" "John!"
"Calm down, hon. I won't put them on."

3.32   Engulfed in Schönberg's cerebral clatter,
John writhes, and looks intensely ill;
Then sits up sharply. "What's the matter?
John—dear," Liz whispers. John says, "Phil!
That's him there—Berkeley—engineering—
His son, too—when we've finished hearing
This horror, let's go say hello."
So in the interval they go
Over to where his friend is showing
His son the rules of tic-tac-toe
On the verso of the program. "Whoa—
Philip, old buddy, how's it going?"
"Not too bad," smiles Phil. "And this is. . . ?"
"Oh, let me introduce you. Liz . . .

3.33   . . . Meet Phil—and Paul—Weiss . . . Liz Dorati."
"Hello." "A pleasure." "Say what, Phil—
The two of us are throwing a party
On Friday night. Housewarming. Will
You join us? Liz has been inviting
Horrendous hordes . . . hey, what's that writing?"
"Nothing," Phil mumbles, "Tic-tac-toe. . . .
If Paul can spare me, sure, I'll go."
"Well, young man, will you free your father?"
"Yes," Paul concedes, "if I can stay
With Chuck Lamont when Dad's away." . . .
"Phil, coffee after this?" "I'd rather
Split following the Brahms. It's late,
And Paul has school at half past eight . . .

3.34   ... This Friday, then.... What was I saying?
Oh, yes, the back of this will do
For your address.... What brilliant playing!
That cellist..." "She's my sister, Sue."
"You're serious?" "Yes." "She's quite amazing.
All four are good, but without raising
Her voice above the others, she
Illuminates the other three.
No stridency, no ostentation,
Clear, moving, fine ... your sister is
A marvelous musician, Liz.
Please pass on my appreciation."
"Tell her yourself on Friday, Phil.
She'd like that." "She'll be there?" "She will."

3.35   John nods, "A word, Phil ... (Liz, excuse us)...
Come early—we two veterans will
Find something crazy to amuse us—
Just like old times." "Old times," says Phil.
John gently says, "Phil, I'm real sorry
About this thing with Claire...." "Don't worry—
These things are for the best. Last week
Our papers came through.... Let's not speak
Of this; instead of an outpouring
Of my disasters, what of you?
What's the worst trauma you've been through?"
"This Schönberg. It's obscenely boring."
"Ah, John, the same cantankerous wit.
My friend, you haven't changed a bit."

3.36   John thinks: "But you've changed . . . your vocation.
Why did you drop your job? If you
Come early for the celebration
We could clear up a thing or two."
He asks, "Phil, how did Datatronics
Take your departure? Histrionics?"
"Oh, no such luck! As soon as I
Checked in my badge and said good-bye,
They took on someone else. . . . But, really
. . . (Phil smiles) . . . to change the subject, Liz
—Your new friend . . . and housewarmer—is
Lovely, I think—although we've merely
Exchanged two words . . . I'm glad for you."
"Thanks, Phil!" John's pleased; and flattered too.

3.37   The lights have dimmed. Now they're returning.
Throats clear. Brahms' A Minor begins.
The brisk allegro. Then a yearning
Warm ductile length of lyric spins
Its lovely glimmering thread at leisure
Inveiglingly from measure to measure
With a continuous tenderness
So deep it smooths out all distress,
All sorrow; ravishing, beguiling . . .
And on and on till silence comes.
Paul whispers, "That's the tune Mom hums!"
Phil's eyes are closed, but Paul is smiling,
Floating on a slow tide of Brahms,
Back in his absent mother's arms.

71

Four

4.1   "Liz, dear, it's been just lovely meeting
      Your friends, and John; what a nice boy.
      We hope that soon. . . ." Without completing
      Her exhortation to enjoy
      A copula more sacramental
      (Resulting in the incidental
      Production of grandchildren—three
      Seems best—to dandle on her knee),
      Mrs. Dorati hugs her daughter
      And drives off with rheumatic care.
      Liz stands and breathes the sharp night air,
      While from the house keen squeals of slaughter
      And wrath attest that Liquid Sheep
      Have just commenced to rant and weep.

4.2   So much for the Vivaldi. Thinking,
"Mom's got out in the nick of time,"
Liz turns back. "Ah, the hostess!" Drinking
His seventh glass of gin and lime,
Professor Pratt, fine-tuned historian
(Renowned creator of *Victorian
Architecture in Pittsburgh; How
Pittsburgh Was Lost and Won*; and now,
With plump grants from the Frosch Foundation
—No less voluminous as he
Hops up the academic tree—
Pittsburgh—The Savior of the Nation),
Roars in her ear as she goes by
And holds her with his bulbous eye.

4.3   "Professor Pratt, how good to meet you . . .
(John's really left me in the lurch) . . ."
"At last, my dear! I thought I'd treat you
To new directions in research
On Pittsburgh." "Thanks, but with this yelling,
Professor Pratt, it would be selling
Your theories short to try . . . (There's John—
That's odd—he's got a new suit on—
And why's he kicking at the table?) . . .
Excuse me. . . ." Liz goes over. "Hi!
Something wrong, dear?" "Yes! just as I
Was hoping things had gotten stable,
As if to prove that all is flux,
Your squalid cat pissed on my tux."

4.4   "Poor Charlemagne. He's agitated.
It's this noise, dear. Please don't make waves."
"Nonsense. That cat should be castrated—
Unless," John splutters, "he behaves...."
"John, dear, don't go all stiff and stuffy.
Look round you. Everyone's so scruffy
A tux looks odd—take my advice.
Oh, by the way, Mom thinks you're nice....
I wonder why Dad couldn't make it...."
Liz ripples on, while John thinks, "Drat
That mangy misbegotten cat.
I hate the beast, and I can't fake it..."
(While Charlemagne, from the back room,
Yowls out symmetric spells of doom.)

4.5   But now with vigor fierce and frantic,
In a new number, "Love Dispriz'd,"
With thuds and screechings corybantic
(The neighbors have been neutralized
By being invited to the frolic),
The Liquid Sheep with hyperbolic
Frenzy are squirming in the spasms
Of uncontrollable orgasms
To Janet's mad, mesmeric drumming....
Then, suddenly, silence. "More! More! More!"
The audience howls for an encore—
But there can be no second coming
For Liquid Sheep, who, mute and spent,
Disband to seek out nourishment.

4.6   Now John keeps Philip circulating.
        "Rose, meet my old friend Philip." Rose
        Finds the Sheep "too, too enervating."
        She smiles at Phil and blows her nose.
        But English unofficial roses
        Are not as bland as he supposes,
        And Rose, whose nasal septum throbs
        With coke, dilates between her sobs
        And snorts, on "Daddy's super bashes";
        Then, wilting from chic gibberish
        Into a bruised Americish:
        "But not all cultural attachés
        Are like my dad, for heaven's sakes!
        Still, that's the way the biscuit breaks."

4.7   Phil frowns, and sets down his manhattan.
        He dips one arm of his thick specs
        —Daubing its tortoiseshell ground pattern
        With bold green guacamole flecks—
        In a nearby bowl, and licks it,
        Massages his blunt nose, and picks it,
        Grunting, "You're really something, chick!"
        He thinks, "If this won't do the trick,
        I'm stuck." But Rose by now is fleeing
        And Phil's left blessedly alone,
        Content in an inviolate zone.
        He chuckles. But alas, Liz, seeing
        Him by himself, steers him to where
        Janet and Sue, with hybrid flair,

4.8   Discuss, "Is acid rock agogic?"
      And "How does Bach relate to punk?"
      As Jan expands with pedagogic
      Verse on the genesis of funk,
      Her new friend states, "*Ein Heldenleben*
      And *Warum ist das Licht gegeben*
      ... (Snatches of which she sings out loud
      —Shy Sue, forgetful of the crowd)...
      Apotheosize pan-Germanic
      Grandeur and gloom...." Phil wishes he
      Could crawl off unobtrusively,
      But heedless of his spiraling panic
      Liz wedges in with "Janet, you
      Know Phil ... Phil, meet my sister, Sue."

4.9   Phil, faced by Janet—Claire's friend—trembles:
      "Hi, Jan, long time no see!" But Jan
      Observes him as if he resembles
      A putrefied orangutan.
      Once Claire and Jan had double-dated
      With Phil and John. Once Claire, elated,
      Stopping her ears to Cabot screams,
      Had wed the pauper of her dreams.
      "Claire's not to blame," thinks Janet stoutly.
      Thus by default the fault is Phil's.
      Jan sets her gaze at Look that Kills
      While Phil admires the floor, devoutly
      Twirling his glass like a prayer wheel,
      And gnaws his lip with vampire zeal.

4.10   Jan says, "Excuse me, Sue. I'll see you."
       Phil's knees feel like papaya pulp.
       Sue asks, "Phil, why did Janet flee you?"
       "Don't know," evades Phil with a gulp:
       "Sue—Sunday night—the 'Royal' trio—
       I thought you played it with great brio. . . ."
       And Sue, diverted, smiles and says,
       "So you were there?" With warm-eyed gaze
       She looks at Phil and thinks, "I wonder
       What it's about—I'm sure John knows—
       He's looking at us—I suppose
       Some unforgotten feud or blunder."
       Across the room, John gloats to Liz,
       "She's falling for him—bet she is!

4.11   We'll get old Phil hitched up, believe me—
       Yes, it's reciprocal—I'm sure—
       Look at his face—he can't deceive me."
       Liz thinks, "That's somewhat premature. . . .
       I'd hardly bounce to that conclusion. . . ."
       Around her, reveling in confusion,
       In attitudes of vague collapse
       Among fruit punch and brandy snaps,
       Her legal colleagues sit discoursing
       With Liquid Sheep and stroke their fleece
       While, leaning on the mantelpiece,
       Frowning, aloof from all this horsing,
       Her brother Ed decants Bordeaux
       On the white woolen rug below.

4.12   Now Bjorn the Swedish runner's leering
At Rose with cold, appraising lust.
She shudders and adjusts an earring.
With reassuring spite and trust
The Van Camps battle on, unthinking:
"No, darling, I have *not* been drinking.
Thanks for the sweet thought, anyway."
"It's nothing, darling. Any day!"
While, bowed down with the gray futility
Of his dank thesis, Kim Tarvesh
Ogles convexities of flesh
And maximizes his utility
By drowning in his chilled Chablis
His economics Ph.D.

4.13   But now Professor Pratt's recaptured
His fugitive, and Liz endures
The bludgeonings of this most enraptured,
Most indefatigable of bores.
He raves of western Pennsylvania
With zealotry approaching mania:
". . . Had we not taken Fort Duquesne,
My dear, the French would still remain
Entrenched in a confederation
From Louisiana to Quebec.
I tell you, Pittsburgh saved our neck—
Pittsburgh—redeemer of our nation!
My fourth book reexamines this.
It's called *The Pratt Hypothesis. . . .*"

4.14   Phil downs vermouth and bourbon, sinking
Out of a world of loss and pain.
He drinks and he continues drinking
And having drunk he drinks again.
Inspired by a warm confusion
In a soft stratum of illusion,
The amber in his glass becomes
A gold elixir that benumbs,
That steadies as it sends him reeling.
A sunflower in a frame of chrome
Reminds him of his childhood home,
And in an access of swift feeling
He sees, with vision like a knife,
Into the very heart of life.

4.15   He thinks of Paul. He thinks . . . John hails him
Across the clouds of smoke-filled air,
Wrestles his way through, and assails him
With "Now that we've achieved this rare
Moment to talk—we'd better use it!
Here's a straight question—don't refuse it—
Why have you left your job?" "To save
The world," replies Phil with a grave
Decorum. "Ah," says John. "Fantastic!
Guess we young yuppies all should go
Do our own thing." Phil murmurs, "Oh—
Young yuppies—now—that's pleonastic. . . ."
"Touché," says John; then, "Phil, you're mad.
What better job could you have had?"

4.16 If John sounds blunt and acrimonious,
It's not surprising. What in Phil
Seemed more refreshing than erroneous
Behavior once, while they were still
At college, now excites causticity.
Phil's amicable eccentricity
Unsettles John now that it's come
To rest a bit too close to home.
Or it may be that, overtaken
By his defensive doubts, he shrinks
Into a quilled attack. Phil thinks:
"John doesn't like his totems shaken.
Before I've threatened him, he fires."
By way of answer, Phil inquires:

4.17 "And your job gives you satisfaction?"
"It's fun—it's well-paid—it's a new
Challenge—" "What is it, John?" "Compaction
Of payloads.... Phil, it can't be true
That you—the whiz kid of computers,
Beloved of bosses as of tutors,
The author of that learned tract
On guidance systems—could in fact
Blow your career—and for dumb slogans."
"To save the world—what's dumb in that?
Before you blow our planet flat
With all your payloads and your blowguns,
We interfering, peace-drugged jerks
Might save your skins—and jinx your works."

4.18   "And how do you propose to do it?"
"Well, Lungless Labs; that's for a start.
We'll picket it, disrupt it, sue it—"
"Phil, Lungless Labs won't give a fart.
They'll slam you straight into the slammer
Where you can practice Russian grammar
Until ... (By ones and twos a knot
Grows round the disputatious spot) ...
Sense penetrates your soft ingenuous
Cerebrum." "John, you've missed the point,"
Says Phil: "The world is out of joint;
And such acts, though they may seem tenuous
To you, give heart to us; what's more,
Bring new peace fodder to our door."

4.19   Speech strained and clarified by passion
    —His S's remain S's still—
In unantagonistic fashion,
Eschewing escalation, Phil
Resumes: "John, take a look around us.
Imagine that the first bombs found us
Just as we are—as here we stand,
A glass of liquor in our hand.
There by the door is Van Gogh's painting
Of sunflowers. Here are all our friends.
And suddenly our small world ends,
And our vile dust is swept up, tainting
The hills, the vineyards, and the seas
With irremediable disease.

4.20   So tell me, how much will it please us
That mankind with its crazy ways
—Bach, Rembrandt, Socrates, and Jesus—
Will burn to ash and swiveling haze?
Will it console us to be knowing
In the swift instant of our going
That Red Square, like our children's crèche,
Will soon be charred or ulcerous flesh?
And then, when the soft radiation
Descends on what's not been destroyed
—Trees, whales, birds, wolves—the birthless void—
Think how the crown of earth's creation
Will murder that which gave him birth,
Ripping out the slow womb of earth.

4.21   Is it just 'we' who feel this terror?
Do you think 'they' can't understand
What will come down through aim or error
Upon their great and fragile land?
We *must* stop—... (Caught by sudden sadness
He fumbles) ...—if we *can*—this madness,
We common people of goodwill...."
A young man stands and stares as Phil
Says, "...Fallout can't tell Omsk from Reno...."
He stands there wordless, half in love,
Drinking Phil's speech, the image of
El Greco's *Felix Paravicino*:
The same pale, slender, passionate face,
Strength and intensity and grace.

4.22 It's Ed. Now Liz has introduced him
       (At his request). Ed, rarely short
       Of words, finds Philip's have reduced him
       To numbness. On the tennis court
       Or with his advertising rabble
       Ed spouts forth a distracting babble
       Of witty entertaining trash
       Till his companions long to smash
       Their rackets on his simmering cranium
       Or seal his lips with editing tape;
       But two sure passwords for escape
       Have been discovered: One's Uranium;
       The other, God. All talk of these
       Causes Ed's babbling brook to freeze.

4.23 Now host and hostess, drawn by duty,
       Have vanished, but—to stay with Ed—
       At twenty-three, though quite astute, he
       Seems easily dispirited;
       Although his energy's appealing,
       It serves the function of concealing `
       Rifts of anxiety so deep
       Some nights he finds it hard to sleep.
       (Liz thinks this trait comes from their mother.)
       Both Sue and Liz adore Ed: he's
       Warmhearted, fun, and quick to please;
       But neither understands their brother
       When his designs and words are skewed
       By what they term his godly mood.

4.24   Phil looks at Ed: intense, athletic,
Silent—the sort of man whom he's
Uneasy with. But Ed's ascetic
Tension betrays his own unease;
And by now Phil's free-floating status
(Buoyed by spirituous afflatus)
Projects goodwill on all mankind—
And so, in half an hour, we find
The pair engaged in conversation,
Which, now that he's regained his cool
And half slipped back to playing the fool,
Revolves round Ed's prolonged narration
Of how he happened to procure
A green iguana from a store.

4.25   "... They had a sale on small iguanas—
Babies—a span long, kind of cute.
Sure, I'd gone in to buy piranhas,
But seeing them, I knew they'd suit
My image: I could take them walking
Through the Financial District, talking
To them about the price of gold.
We wouldn't make the centerfold
Of *Playgirl*, as they aren't too pretty,
But what the heck, I didn't care:
Traffic would swerve, and folks would stare
—I had it figured out—the city
Would halt, the cops would come and say,
'Get those darn things out of the way!'

4.26   But, sadly, Arnold Schwarzenegger
       —I got just one—looks really strange:
       His legs keep getting bigger and bigger
       But not his torso—Should I change
       His food?" Ed asks with some disquiet
       "Don't know," replies Phil. "What's his diet?"
       "Salads, and larvae—and bonemeal."
       "Why that?" asks Phil. "Because I feel
       His jaw's so rubbery and floppy
       He may need extra calcium." "No.
       The phosphorus-calcium ratio
       Is far too high in bonemeal. Copy
       My method: cut that bonemeal out,
       And feed it vitamins till it's stout.

4.27   To feed it bonemeal is to maim it."
       "You've kept iguanas, Phil?" "Oh, sure—
       Iguanas, rabbits, dogs, you name it!
       My wife—but I don't any more . . .
       (Phil's speech grows slurred) . . . We got a spider—
       Paul and I call it Easy Rider."
       "Who's Paul?" "My son. He lives with me."
       Ed frowns at Phil: "Why shouldn't he?"
       "Oh! I'm divorced," says Phil. "You married?"
       "No, no—" "Well, don't! Women are turds.
       That whole snake pit is . . . for the birds,"
       Phil mutters—but his slurs have carried
       To Jan, who with ferocious mien
       Injects herself into the scene.

4.28 "Phil, you're obnoxious . . . (Like a razor
   Her voice dissects him) . . . when you're drunk."
   Her eyes bore through him like a laser.
   "What. . . ? What. . . ?" In an amnesic funk,
   "What did I say?" asks Philip (thinking,
   That's Jan . . . she's pretty nice . . . likes drinking . . .
   What's made her mad?) ". . . Hey, have a drink—"
   He offers her a glass. "Men stink!"
   Janet exclaims with tingling fury.
   "You puke all over us, then say,
   'What did I do?' file us away
   As saint, virago, nag, slut, houri
   Or household pet or household drudge—
   God—Claire was right. . . ." Phil does not budge

4.29 From where Jan leaves him, rooted, staring.
   He leans in foggy shock on Ed.
   Then in a voice drunk and despairing:
   "I'm plastered! What was it I said?"
   "Nothing you meant. You're right. You're plastered."
   "I'm going . . . home. . . ." "Unless you've mastered
   The art of driving straight when drunk,
   Once you're behind that wheel, you're sunk!
   I'll drive you home. Come back tomorrow
   To fetch—" "I live near Stanford, Ed."
   "Oh . . . well, in that case, share my bed—
   Just don't try driving!—You can borrow
   My toothbrush too. Come on, let's go—
   Good night, Liz—Bye, John—Homeward ho!"

4.30 They totter car-wards. Now Ed's driving
      Toward his spartan lodgings, where,
      Within two minutes of arriving,
      Stretched on the bed, Phil sees a chair
      Piled high with shirts, a tennis racket,
      A Bible, an unopened packet
      Of guitar strings, a saxophone,
      Shaving cream, razor and cologne. . . .
      A commentary on Aquinas
      Rests on the floor, while on a shelf
      Lies the august *Summa* itself,
      Next to (in order) *Conquering Shyness,*
      The Zen of Chess, The Eightfold Way,
      Theories of Film, and the *Pensées.*

4.31 Phil looks around at Ed's housekeeping.
      Ed yawns, and strips off shirt and shoes.
      Silence outside. The iguana's sleeping.
      This quiet grid of avenues
      With red-flowered gum for decoration
      Lies deep in slumber and sedation.
      "It suits me, Phil. The flat's quite small,
      But there's a garden, after all—
      And a small pool for the iguana. . . ."
      Phil's bleary eyes rest on a bowl
      Of fruit, a crucifix, a roll
      Of film, a photograph of Lana
      Turner, who smiles across the floor
      At Holbein's sketch of Thomas More.

4.32   "My patron saint." "Which one?" Ed, grinning,
         Says, "Go to sleep!" and turns to pray.
         He asks forgiveness for his sinning,
         Gives thanks for the expended day,
         Consigns his spirit to God's charity. . . .
         Now Philip, with exiguous clarity
         And some bewilderment, sees Ed
         Cross himself twice, then come to bed.
         Lights out. Phil mumbles, "What a party!
         I really blew it then with Jan.
         Ed, thanks a lot. I mean it, man—
         I haven't yet met a Dorati
         I didn't like . . . (Across the bed
         He reaches out and touches Ed) . . .

4.33   . . . Good night." Ed fears to answer. Trembling,
         He moves his hand across the space
         —What terrifying miles—assembling
         His courage, touches Philip's face
         And feels him tense up and go rigid.
         "I'm sorry," Ed says, in a frigid,
         Half-choking voice, "I thought you might—
         I didn't mean—I mean—good night."
         Taut with a cataleptic tension
         They lie, unspeaking. Phil thinks, "Why
         Be so uptight? He's a great guy.
         I've never bothered with convention.
         God! It's a year that I've been chaste. . . ,"
         And puts his arm around Ed's waist.

4.34   Now, just as things were getting tenser,
And Ed and Phil were making love,
The imperial official censor
—Officious and imperious—drove
His undiscriminating panzer
Straight through the middle of my stanza.
Now, Gentle Reader, is it right
This swine should put my Muse to flight,
Rooting about among my pearly
Wisdom till he finds orts that he
Can gobble down with grunting glee?
Forgive me, Reader, if I'm surly
At having to replace the bliss
I'd hoped I could portray, with this.

4.35   I'll move the ménage to mañana,
But under protest. Saturday
Dawns bright and clear, and the iguana
—Fantastic dragon of green clay,
Great saurian from realms primeval!—
With scraping, scuffling, and upheaval
Bestirs himself now in his shed.
Ed yawns and half gets out of bed,
Returns and nuzzles Philip's shoulder,
Puts on his jeans, and goes to get
An avocado for his pet.
He says, "Poor Schwarz. It's getting colder.
This heat's kaput. Tonight instead,
You can sleep underneath the bed."

4.36   The warty beast observes Ed coldly,
Stares at the green and mottled pear
He proffers. Noisily and boldly
He crawls toward him, unaware
Of the loose leash that Ed is holding.
Ed slips it round him, gently scolding:
"Now watch that dewlap—mind those spines—"
But Schwarzenegger undermines
All of Ed's efforts at persuasion
—By jerking, clawing—until he
Obtains his avocado. "We
Are now prepared for an invasion
Of our quiescent neighborhood.
You want a walk? ... (The head bobs.) ... Good!"

4.37   Ed leaves, upon the kitchen table,
A note: *Dear Phil, Please help yourself*
To breakfast. Sorry I'm not able
To make it. Coffee's on the shelf.
I'll be back soon. Ed and his lizard
Now do their rounds: a comely wizard
And his unsightly basilisk.
Behind, two neighbors' children risk
Utter and prompt annihilation
Should the familiar's fiendish eyes
Turn on them. "You'll burn up," Pam cries.
She quakes in fear and veneration.
"Coward!" says Gabrielle in a tone
Of scorn. "You'll only turn to stone ...

4.38   You scaredy cat!" Pam begins crying.
        Swiftly the reptile eyes look back.
        Gabrielle gasps. Pam, petrifying,
        Awaits the fiery-tongued attack.
        "Hello," says Ed, "meet my iguana,
        Brought all the way from Ecbatana
        In the mysterious land of Wales
        For kids to stroke his shiny scales."
        Pam thaws to Ed's enlightened coaching:
        "Here's how to pet the friendly beast.
        He isn't slimy in the least."
        Pam frowns and touches him, reproaching
        Her friend (who's having none of that)
        With "Yeah? Now who's a scaredy cat!"

4.39   Perfecting their aerobic labors,
        Once more around the block they creep,
        Greeted by mailmen and by neighbors.
        When Ed returns, Phil's still asleep.
        But, upon waking, to his credit,
        He does not try to expunge or edit
        —With, "Geez, I had so much to drink
        Last night, I really cannot think
        What happened . . ."—what in fact transpired.
        He smiles at Ed: "Good morning." "Hi!
        Coffee?" "You bet." Ed's somewhat shy.
        "This coffee really gets you wired,"
        Phil says. "It's just like . . . (With a groan) . . .
        Christ! Paul! Ed, may I use your phone?"

4.40 "Sure. Phil—if Paul has no objection—
Would you—I've got this weekend free...."
Phil dials, nods, gets the connection.
"Joan? This is Phil. Is Paul—I see—
I'll wait.... Hi, son, how are things going?—
Chuck's baseball cap? Great!—So they're showing
What? *Star Wars*? No, I can't allow—
Now, young man, don't you teach me how....
Paul! Did you hear me? *Star Wars*—Never!—
I don't care what she lets him do—
What's that? Chuck will make fun of you?—
Well, just this once then—But don't ever...
(Alas! that such Affected Tricks
Should flourish in a Child of Six!)

4.41 ...You're welcome—You're a tricky fellow—
Does Monday suit you?—You don't care?...
(Phil laughs)...You're having fun!—Don't bellow:
It sounds worse than a madhouse there—
See you then, son—No, nothing, staying
With a friend—Ed—yeah, that's right, playing!....
(Phil shakes his head)...Now give the phone
To Mrs. Lamont...Hello there, Joan.
Thanks for all this—Not Sunday, Monday,
Yes, after school—Yes, he can see
Star Wars—Say hi to Matt for me!—
That's very kind. I hope that one day
I can take care of Chuck for you
When you've got other things to do."

4.42   The weekend kicks off with a glorious
Brunch at an open-air café.
Champagne and omelettes. Ed's censorious
Conscience is dormant for a day.
They drive across to Sausalito;
Later, divide a vile burrito
From Taco Hut, and wash it down
With a Dos Equis, cool and brown.
Ed suggests tennis next, and trounces
His friend with effortless panache;
To cool themselves they take a splash
In Schwarz's pool, where Phil denounces
Schwarz as the dullest, dimmest, and
Least soulful beast of sea or land.

4.43   The iguana stares: obtuse, phlegmatic,
Full five feet long from tail to snout,
He complements Ed's sharp, erratic
Essence (as wurst does sauerkraut).
With evening, Ed and Phil go walking
Through the calm city—laughing, talking;
A mentor's what Ed needs; and Phil,
Warm and Socratic, fits the bill.
At night, Ed brings in his iguana.
Phil eyes him warily, while he
Eyes Philip just as warily.
Phil tries to bribe him. A banana?
The monster bloats his jowls at this,
Emitting his hoarse gular hiss.

4.44   "Phil, don't annoy him." "The causation
Should run from him to me instead . . .
But I suppose I'm on probation.
Where will he sleep?" "Beneath our bed."
"Beneath our *bed*? His least vibration
Will rock the room to its foundation."
"Don't slander Schwarz." "Well, on your head
Be it if one of us is dead
By dawn—" "It's just for the duration
That the heat's knocked out in his shed.
I'll fix it. If it's cold," says Ed,
"And Schwarz goes into hibernation,
It could be months. . . ." The quadruped
Advances now with torpid tread.

4.45   They sleep. (There is no other option.)
Their ectothermic chaperone,
Taking to his in-house adoption,
Sinks into slumber like a stone.
Ed goes next day to church, confession;
He strays home with a lost expression,
And mumbles, "Phil . . . I don't know quite
If what we're doing is . . . is right."
"What do you mean?" asks Philip, puzzled:
"We both—" "I know," says Ed at length,
"I've prayed to God to give us strength
To—Phil, I—Oh my God, I've muzzled
Love's only true voice, Jesus Christ,
Who came to earth and sacrificed

4.46   His life for me ... for me, a sinner."
Phil looks at Ed, then says, "My friend,
Let's fix that heating. After dinner
We'll talk this out." But dinner's end
Sees Ed in new heart altogether,
As if a cloudburst of black weather
Had been dispersed and, rinsed by storm,
The night is generous and warm.
Phil looks at his good-looking lover's
Face as he prays: its casque of peace
Cleansed of all turbulent caprice
And guilt, and, as they pull the covers
Over themselves, says, "Ed, I'm glad
For these three evenings that we've had. . . ."

4.47   What does Phil see in Ed? Why does he
Seem so committed to him? True,
Once at a party, drunk and fuzzy
—John should be shaken if he knew—
Phil made it with a guy at college.
(Well, once or twice.) And he'd acknowledge,
Even when married, now and then,
His eye might stray toward other men.
But that's it. And, though unconventional,
That too seems meager cause why he
Should fall for Ed so speedily.
Not that affection is intentional
Or that, in matters of the heart,
We should pull leaf and leaf apart. . . .

4.48   But still: Phil's always been attracted
         By vulnerable people; Ed,
         Eager, confused, intent, abstracted,
         Is passionate in both speech and bed.
         How good it is to be admired;
         And how much more to be desired!
         Ed's restlessnesses, sudden calms,
         And, as he lies in Philip's arms,
         His sad and serious expression
         Affect Phil more than he can say.
         Thus, in a strange, contagious way,
         Ed's very lack of self-possession
         Reduces Phil's, and so destroys
         The outer suburbs of his poise.

4.49   Next morning, at first light, Ed, waking,
         Kneels down in silence on the floor.
         A calm and chilly dawn is breaking
         Over the bay. As his first chore,
         He goes to nurture his iguana
         With three persimmons, a sultana,
         Some lettuce, and an unripe yam
         (A favorite, with a dab of jam).
         Now Phil awakens from his coma:
         "Monday! I guess I'd better call
         The Peaceniks, then head south for Paul."
         They drive down to the Café Soma
         (On 12th and Howard, close to where
         Ed works); and order breakfast there.

4.50   Over large cups of coffee, steaming
And fragrant, Ed says, "Phil, last night
I almost thought that I was dreaming.
But now—I know it wasn't right.
I have to trust my faith's decisions,
Not batten on my own volitions.
The Bible says, if a man lie
With a man, he must surely die.
It's in Leviticus, chapter 20,
Verse 13—which means it's as true
For me, a Christian, as for you."
Phil laughs: "That old book, Ed, holds plenty
Of rules that may have made sense once
—Take shellfish—but you'd be a dunce

4.51   To trim your heart by its sharp letter.
That kills, as someone sometime said.
What's wrong with sex? The more the better
If you like someone." Flushing red,
Ed frowns and says, "Don't bring in shellfish.
That's trivial. . . . How can I be selfish
And lust for flesh instead of truth?
It's like a kid with a sweet tooth
On a no-sugar diet breaking
Into a cookie store for me
To put myself where I can be . . ."
"Tempted?" prompts Phil: "No point my taking
Exception to your version of
Who first suggested making love."

4.52   "Phil—please—don't . . . how can I explain it?
        The point is that my body is
        Not mine alone—I don't disdain it—
        But it's God's instrument—my bliss
        Is in his will—and its perfection
        Resides in love, whose chief projection
        Is to give life. All other use
        Falls short of this. It is abuse
        Even if lovers feel they're loving.
        When our will fails, we've got to pray,
        'Help thou my unbelief.' That way . . ."
        "That's bullshit. Ed, what are you proving?
        That two men or two women don't . . ."
        "Phil, try to understand." "I won't.

4.53   I can't . . . (His voice shakes.) . . . You were saying,
        Before I interrupted, God
        Will help our unbelief, our fraying
        Resolve. But what was wrong or odd
        With last night's loveliness between us?
        Given a God, if he had seen us
        And he is just and loving-kind,
        Why should you think that he would mind
        My touch, your trembling, our caresses,
        The loving smart in your clear eyes,
        My hands ruffling your hair, our sighs?
        If anything, I'd say he blesses
        The innocent bodies that express
        So forthrightly such happiness.

4.54   That's how I feel. But for the lecture
        And weekend, thank you, Ed." His eyes
        Meet Ed's, and with a sad conjecture
        Ed asks, "We'll keep in touch?" They rise.
        "Sure, sure," Phil mumbles. "You can write me."
        Ed says, "Phil, why don't you invite me
        Down to your place sometime perhaps?"
        "Yes, anytime, feel free. . . ." They lapse
        Into a bitter silence. Gilding
        The great bole of a churchyard oak
        The angled sun now shifts to soak
        With liquid light Ed's office building,
        Near which, with nothing more to say,
        The two shake hands and turn away.

Five

5.1 A week ago, when I had finished
Writing the chapter you've just read
And with avidity undiminished
Was charting out the course ahead,
An editor—at a plush party
(Well-wined, -provisioned, speechy, hearty)
Hosted by (long live!) Thomas Cook
Where my Tibetan travel book
Was honored—seized my arm: "Dear fellow,
What's your next work?" "A novel . . ." "Great!
We hope that you, dear Mr. Seth—"
". . . In verse," I added. He turned yellow.
"How marvelously quaint," he said,
And subsequently cut me dead.

5.2   Professor, publisher, and critic
      Each voiced his doubts. I felt misplaced.
      A writer is a mere arthritic
      Among these muscular Gods of Taste.
      As for that sad blancmange, a poet—
      The world is hard; he ought to know it.
      Driveling in rhyme's all very well;
      The question is, does spittle sell?
      Since staggering home in deep depression,
      My will's grown weak. My heart is sore.
      My lyre is dumb. I have therefore
      Convoked a morale-boosting session
      With a few kind if doubtful friends
      Who've asked me to explain my ends.

5.3   How do I justify this stanza?
      These feminine rhymes? My wrinkled muse?
      This whole passé extravaganza?
      How can I (careless of time) use
      The dusty bread molds of Onegin
      In the brave bakery of Reagan?
      The loaves will surely fail to rise
      Or else go stale before my eyes.
      The truth is, I can't justify it.
      But as no shroud of critical terms
      Can save my corpse from boring worms,
      I may as well have fun and try it.
      If it works, good; and if not, well,
      A theory won't postpone its knell.

5.4   Why, asks a friend, attempt tetrameter?
Because it once was noble, yet
Capers before the proud pentameter,
Tyrant of English. I regret
To see this marvelous swift meter
Demean its heritage, and peter
Into mere Hudibrastic tricks,
Unapostolic knacks and knicks.
But why take all this quite so badly?
I would not, had I world and time
To wait for reason, rhythm, rhyme
To reassert themselves, but sadly
The time is not remote when I
Will not be here to wait. That's why.

5.5   Reader, enough of this apology;
But spare me if I think it best,
Before I tether my monology,
To stake a stanza to suggest
You spend some unfilled day of leisure
By that original spring of pleasure:
Sweet-watered, fluent, clear, light, blithe
(This homage merely pays a tithe
Of what in joy and inspiration
It gave me once and does not cease
To give me)—Pushkin's masterpiece
In Johnston's luminous translation:
Eugene Onegin—like champagne
Its effervescence stirs my brain.

5.6 . . . But back to Ed. It's Monday. Seven.
   Day's over at the office grind.
   Ed walks back to his car. To leaven
   The sadness that besets his mind
   He broods on coffee. Should he favor
   The brand name of Encore or Savor?
   What tag, what label would work best?
   What media strategy? Depressed,
   He drops a quarter to a wino,
   Stands by a storefront shirt display,
   Observes his hair in disarray
   And smooths it absently. "Well, I know
   I'll never hear from him again,"
   He thinks with unaccustomed pain.

5.7 It's dark. He drives. The street lamps glimmer
   Through cooling air. The golden globes
   By City Hall glow, and the glimmer
   —Like sequins on black velvet robes—
   Of lights shines out across the water,
   Across the bay, unruffled daughter
   Of the Pacific; on the crests
   Of hill and bridge red light congests
   The sky with rubies. Briskly blinking,
   Planes—Venus-bright—traverse the sky.
   Ed drives on, hardly knowing why,
   Across the tall-spanned bridge. Unthinking,
   He parks, and looks out past the strait,
   The deep flood of the Golden Gate.

5.8   Subdued and silent, he surveys it—
       The loveliest city in the world.
       No veiling words suffice to praise it,
       But if you saw it as, light-pearled,
       Fog-fingered, pinnacled, I see it
       Across the black tide, you'd agree it
       Outvied the magic of your own.
       Even tonight, as Ed, alone,
       Makes out Marina, plaza, tower,
       Fort Point, Presidio—he feels
       A benediction as it steals
       Over his heart with its still power.
       He thinks, "I'll phone Phil. No, instead,
       Better to write him, as he said."

5.9   He drives home, feeds Schwarz, starts inditing
       The fragment reproduced below.
       He shakes his head, stares at his writing:
       Dear Phil, Forgive me, I don't know
       How you'll react when you receive this.
       Perhaps you'll think, "I don't believe this.
       We talked for two whole days. What could
       Be left that I've misunderstood?"
       Let me explain, Phil, my position. . . .
       Ed, muttering, "This won't do at all,"
       Crumples the sheet into a ball,
       Lobs his uneloquent petition
       Into a corner of his room,
       And sinks back into hamstrung gloom.

5.10   Something has stung Ed's heart so badly
        That now he wends his quipless way
        From home to work to home so sadly
        (Without the energy to play
        Guitar or tennis or the jester)
        That all his office buddies pester
        Him to reveal his cause of woe.
        When Ed replies he doesn't know,
        It's only partially evasion.
        The truth is, Ed's himself unclear.
        As a strict rule he's tried to steer
        Away from men of Phil's persuasion.
        From common funds of lore he's learned:
        "Fall for a bi, and you'll get burned."

5.11   Why is it then that Ed, unshielded
        From passion's fallout (or attacked
        By Cupid's minutemen), has yielded
        His heart to Phil? The very fact
        That Phil was married, and is living
        With his young son, succeeds in giving
        Him the attraction, in Ed's eyes,
        Of someone sound and worldly-wise.
        Will Phil provide him with direction?
        Could Ed's long quest be at an end?
        Is Phil, at last, "that special friend"?
        But how, Ed wonders in dejection,
        Even if they do meet, can he
        Make Phil consent to chastity?

5.12   A month goes by. Ed's tennis-playing
       Resumes. His quips resume. He works
       Efficiently, without betraying
       The intermittent pain that lurks
       Below his smile by day, appearing
       In his dark eyes as night is nearing.
       He feels that there's no hope at all,
       Yet waits in hope that Phil might call,
       And once or twice he's almost lifted
       The telephone to ring his friend,
       Or tried to write, but in the end
       The common doubt of those born gifted
       With his uncommon looks prevails
       And his unfixed intention fails.

5.13   At length, instead of phone or letter,
       He thinks, "I ought to visit Sue.
       I missed her concert, and I'd better
       Redeem myself...." Without ado,
       One Friday afternoon, arriving
       After an hour of freeway driving
       At Sue's door with his pet in train,
       He kisses her. "Hi, sis!" In vain
       Does Sue with chess, Casals, and cooking
       Try to restrain her restive guest.
       At six o'clock he flies the nest.
       "Sue, help me out with this. I'm looking
       For an address on Cowper Street—"
       "Who's is it?" "Phil's. We ... said we'd meet."

5.14   Phil and his son, while cooking dinner,
        Play tic-tac-toe. But sharp-eyed Paul,
        Who sees that there can be no winner
        When players know the game at all,
        Says, "Teach me chess, Dad." Phil is worried.
        "Such things," he thinks, "should not be hurried.
        The boy's too bright for his own good.
        Would Claire . . . would Spock suggest I should
        Encourage him in this precocity?
        He could become within a week
        A wide-eyed fianchetto freak—
        And yet, to crush his curiosity. . . ."
        But suddenly, with knock and din,
        Ed and companion tumble in.

5.15   "Ed!" "Dad, what's that?" "Phil, I'm intruding,
        I know, but—" "No, you're not, sit down.
        Just chain that brute up." "You're alluding
        To Schwarzenegger?" "Yes, you clown.
        Can't you see Paul's scared?" "I'm not, really—
        Dad—promise—" Paul says insincerely.
        "Paul, this is Ed." "Hi, Ed." "And this
        Is my iguana." With a hiss
        The beast completes the introduction.
        "So, Ed, what brings you here today?"
        Ed misconstrues his hopes to say
        —Half scared himself of misconstruction—
        "I've just dropped by to see if you . . .
        I mean, I'm really visiting Sue."

5.16   "Well, stay and eat." "Sure?" "Do you doubt me?"
Paul breaks in with "Ed, teach me chess!"
"I guess you two can do without me,"
Says Phil with magnified distress:
"I'd better go and warm the dishes."
Ed, catering promptly to Paul's wishes
(For all Doratis, after all,
Wallowed in chess when they were small
And harbor no inane compunctions
About the burdened infant brain),
Talks of black rooks, white knights, profane
Bishops, the monarch's leisured functions,
Passed pawns—tsarinas *soi-disant*—
And sidelong butchery *en passant*.

5.17   Paul's eyes expand. His small head's bubbling
At this grand glimpse of a new world.
Dumb at his master's feet, not troubling
His discourse, somnolently curled,
The iguana gently heaves, completing
The Dutch interior. While they're eating
From time to time Phil looks at Ed,
Who flushes a dark rapid red.
Paul falls asleep, still at the table.
Phil carries him to bed. "Not ill—
Just tired—overtaxed." When Phil
Returns, Ed says, "I'm glad you're able
To bear my company at all."
"What do you mean?" "I meant to call—

5.18 Or write, Phil—but the thought obsessed me . . .
(Ed looks down) . . . that you liked—I mean—
I don't know—but it still depressed me—
I've been around gay bars—that scene
Where if you're handsome, people paw you
—I guess you've never had them claw you
As if you were a hunk of meat . . .
(Phil frowns) . . . but—Phil, let me complete
What I—I mean—" Phil's mind is reeling.
He cuts in: "I don't understand.
What's your point, Ed?" (He takes his hand.)
Ed says, "I guess it's just a feeling—
That you just like—a fear, I guess—"
"That I just like your body?" "Yes."

5.19 "I like it, sure." "See what I told you?"
"Ed, go upgrade your personal file.
Your superego's undersold you.
You're a nice guy as well. Don't smile
So wryly. There's no doubt about it.
But all this talk—let's do without it.
This vivisection hurts my head.
I say we ought to go to bed.
We seem to sort things out much better
When horizontal . . . hey, don't blush!"
Ed stands: "I'm sorry—got to rush—
I promised Sue—" "Well, I won't fetter
This fine fraternal flair and fuss,
But come have breakfast here with us.

5.20   And ask Sue too." Six kinds of cereal,
Waffles and syrup, sausage, jam,
Scrambled eggs, French toast—an imperial
Repast next morning—bacon, ham,
Hot coffee, quiche, cream cheese and bagels,
Brie, fruit, banana bread—inveigles
The appetite of each potluck guest
Who at the sovereign behest
Of Mrs. Craven, organizer
Of Phil's Alfresco Breakfasts, comes
To bloat himself until he numbs
His sense and palate—and supplies her
With a like moiety to share
With old friends in the open air.

5.21   A (criminal) lawyer and a (civil)
Engineer talk of safety laws;
A (moral) philosopher of the Devil
While angel cake melts in his jaws.
Her red locks graced with a camellia,
Rowena stands and bats her cilia.
Anne Gunn, the artist, wields her fork
With graphic verve, impaling pork.
Beneath the heavy-branched magnolia
The din of decibels grows dense.
Phil, seeing, backed against a fence,
Ed sunk in sullen melancholia
Among this crush of strangers, walks
Over to him, and smiles, and talks.

5.22   "Two mornings each month—alternating
Sabbaths for Christians and for Jews—
We hold these breakfasts, celebrating
—Hi, Joan, hi, Matt—Ed, please excuse
Me just a—I see Chuck is playing
With Paul again—as I was saying,
To celebrate—but, Ed, where's Sue?"
"At home. She says hello to you—
Jan and her cronies from the city
Are coming for a couple days.
Stanford's museum, you know, displays
Some fine Rodins—" "Well, it's a pity."
"But celebrating what?" "Oh yes—
Just that we're still alive, I guess!"

5.23   "Phil, isn't that a bit excessive?"
"Well, actually, it's an excuse
To meet and eat—but it's impressive
How much we get done. Grapefruit juice?
Look, Ed, stop nibbling and start eating—
Yes, you! Your empty plate's defeating
The purpose of this enterprise. . . .
I see Rowena's making eyes
At—better watch out—once she falls for
Someone—across a crowded room
Or even here—it's certain doom.
She's looking your way now! This calls for
Evasive . . . too late! By my thumbs,
Ed-wards the guided missile comes. . . ."

5.24   . . . Hi, Krakatoa, how's it going?"
       "Hello, Phil—who's your friend?" "Ed." "Hi!"
       Miss Craven, with her coiffure glowing
       Into the startled morning sky,
       Pinches Ed's ass from friendly habit.
       Ed, like a schizophrenic rabbit,
       Ekes out a terror-stricken smile.
       And now, with her beguiling guile,
       Rowena, after politicking
       For strategy versus Lungless Labs,
       Swerves: "Phil, I know you're up for grabs
       Today. I'm going olive-picking.
       I want you—and your cute friend here—
       To join me." And she tweaks Ed's ear.

5.25   "Sorry, Rowena dear, I'm busy."
       "You're not. I've asked your son." "Ah . . . well,
       Rowena, I've been feeling dizzy.
       I ought to lie down for a spell."
       "Nonsense. A brisk walk's just what's needed.
       You'll feel much better once you've heeded
       My unprofessional advice,
       Practical, priceless, and precise.
       I am, you know, a doctor's daughter.
       Besides, Paul, Chuck, Matt, Joan, and Mum
       Are coming, so you've got to come!"
       Thus undermined, as calves to slaughter,
       Stripped of all reasonable recourse,
       Phil and Ed yield to matchless force.

112

5.26   "Where's Schwarz?" Phil humors Ed, who's glowering.
        "Back in the car." "Let's let him out."
        On the back seat the iguana's cowering.
        At Ed's approach he flails about
        With his long tail in fierce frustration.
        Ed leaps back with an imprecation.
        Only when pacified with quiche
        Does the green beast receive his leash.
        Yet, smarting still from the indignity
        Of his incarceration, Schwarz
        Lunges and jerks in fits and starts
        Of uninhibited malignity
        (Bobbing his head in truculent show)
        At guests as they prepare to go.

5.27   Anne Gunn, who draws delight from sketching
        The unearthlier products of the earth,
        Decides that Schwarz is "rather fetching."
        The others give him wider berth.
        Some leave to play football or footsie,
        Some for a matinee of *Tootsie*,
        To watch a high school tennis match
        Or tend their vegetable patch,
        Study statistics, skunks, or Serbia,
        Shop, sail, or swive, stretch out and snooze,
        Or smoke a joint, or strum the blues,
        Repair the doodads of suburbia,
        Plan out the Lungless Labs campaign,
        Or dream of real estate in Spain.

5.28   Paul and the three Lamonts, Rowena
        And Mrs. Craven, Phil, and Ed
        Are left. Phil hums a sonatina
        While lyrics from the Grateful Dead
        Pour out in imitation finer
        Than ever parakeet or mynah
        Accomplished, from the lesser red-
        Capped Craven. Now from the homestead
        They've sallied forth with poles and plastic
        Trash bags (unused) to Campus Drive
        Where rows of olive trees survive
        —Gnarled, silver-shimmering—the drastic
        Legions of cars that foul the street
        With the vile vapors they excrete.

5.29   Now Chuck and Paul are sternly slaying
        Space monsters in the olive trees.
        Below them, Matt Lamont, displaying
        Ornithological expertise,
        Mild-manneredly remarks, "No, darling,
        That's not a grackle, that's a starling.
        It's just got grime upon its coat."
        Matt and Joan claim that they'll devote
        Their lives, once they've retired at forty,
        To "birds and orchids" (Private joke:
        Birds and/or kids—significant stroke).
        He calls her cultural and haughty
        And horticultural—while she,
        Maintaining green-thumbed dignity,

5.30   Backs her belief in cultivation
       With the most brilliant plot in miles:
       Aristocratic conflagration
       Of standard roses; fragrant isles:
       Lemongrass, lemon balm, and lemon
       Geranium; pear and persimmon;
       Fat orchids by the live-oak tree:
       Rich, various, all in harmony;
       No mean feat for a pediatrician
       (Full time) with son and home to boot
       And (each way) half an hour's commute.
       Her husband, Matt, is Phil's physician,
       Addict of crossword, bird, and pun
       And second father to Phil's son.

5.31   The iguana with delight arboreal,
       Pacific in the olive boughs,
       Lies basking. But with gladiatorial
       Proddings the Space Invaders rouse
       Him from his sweet siesta. Shaking
       With shock, with fear and fury quaking,
       He drops down six feet to the ground
       While round him hoodlum hoots resound.
       As he withdraws to Ed's protection,
       Rowena laughs: "Schwarz ought to be
       The emblem of World Amity."
       Ed grunts, "I don't see the connection."
       "Well, for a start, rather than fight
       Violence with violence, Schwarz takes flight.

5.32   Besides, his species of iguana
      Is just as difficult to find
      In Moscow, Washington, Havana,
      And Bonn: he's truly nonaligned.
      A creature of herbivorous habit,
      He wouldn't wish to harm a rabbit.
      His bloodless vegetable love,
      Vaster than empires, ought to move
      Mankind to less carnivorous custom.
      Lastly, he shows—he chose a spot
      With olive branches—how, if not
      To love our enemies, to trust 'em.
      In short, in deed, thought, sign, and soul
      He'd honor his symbolic role."

5.33   Before Ed can respond, a clamor
      Breaks forth above. Ed hears Chuck say,
      "You're my *worst* friend." The brittle glamour
      Of allied triumph's given way
      To a postbellum fit of feuding.
      Paul growls, with Achillean brooding,
      "I killed him first." "No, it was me."
      Irreconcilability
      Threatens to lead to total breakdown,
      But when Matt shouts, "You shrikes, don't shirk—"
      The foes, in common dread of work,
      Are reconciled and, as they shake down
      Strings of black fruit from the ripe tree,
      Are captured by Matt's kodakry.

5.34 From irresponsible flirtation
   Aimed at the irresponsive Ed,
   Rowena, Queen of Machination,
   Now moves to soap up Phil instead.
   Alas, unlathered by her blathering,
   Phil concentrates on olive-gathering.
   His hands incarnadined with juice,
   His shirt-sleeves dark with pulp and puce,
   He toils with sweat-drenched brow and collar,
   Humming, but without let or lag
   Stripping the fruit from twig to bag
   Till he hears Mrs. Craven holler,
   "That's all, folks. We've got three bags full.
   So let's go home, and gather wool."

5.35 And so they do. The fruit lie soaking,
   Immersed in water in her tub,
   And Mrs. Craven, laughing, smoking,
   And gesturing with her cigar stub,
   In undejected recollection
   Talks of her husband, with affection
   Revamping her black-humored joke
   Of how he died though she would smoke.
   "Rowena, you're just like your father—
   You worry that the world will end.
   What if the heavens do descend
   On Chicken Little's head? I'd rather
   Not fret my whole existence through
   When there's so little I can do."

5.36   Late in the afternoon, out walking,
        Phil says to Ed, "Rowena seems
        Quite keen on you. Why are you balking?"
        "She doesn't figure in my dreams.
        Your chest's the one she wants to lean on,"
        States Ed: "But even if she's keen on
        Me—which I doubt—women, I find,
        Don't turn me on." "Christ, what a bind!"
        Phil laughs. "You're like a starving pigeon
        Who just can't bring himself to eat
        Barley or rice, yet thinks the wheat
        He likes is poisoned. Your religion
        Doesn't square too well with your lust.
        I wonder which first bites the dust!"

5.37   "You find that funny?" "No, not really."
        "Why did you say what you just said?"
        "I didn't mean to mock. I merely
        Enjoyed the contradiction, Ed.
        Things puzzling, contrary, or ironic
        Revivify me like a tonic—
        And inexplicabilities
        Accost us even from the trees.
        Look—there's my favorite 'conference maple,'
        Of all the many hundreds, one
        Where at the setting of the sun
        Birds congregate—as if by papal
        Fiat a chattering conclave
        Of cardinals crammed a narrow nave."

5.38   Despite himself, Ed grins. "You're pretty
       Free with your similes today.
       Because your sacrilege is witty
       This time I'll let you get away.
       Watch out, though, if your wit gets grosser—"
       But now, as they're approaching closer,
       The hubbub's risen to a pitch
       That makes their pelted eardrums twitch
       And pulverizes conversation.
       The birds are screaming, and the pair,
       Awed by their ardor, stand and stare.
       Incomprehensible elation
       Floods through their spirits, as the light
       Dies with the sound, and it is night.

5.39   Dark night and silent, calm, and lovely,
       That stills the efforts of our lives,
       Rare, excellent-kind, and behovely . . .
       No matter how the poet strives
       To weave with epithets and clauses
       Your soundless web, he falters, pauses,
       And your enchantment slips between
       His hands, as if it's never been.
       Of all times most imbued with beauty,
       You lend us by your spell relief
       From ineradicable grief
       (If for a spell), and pain, and duty.
       We sleep, and nightly are made whole
       In all our fretted mind and soul.

5.40   They walk, not daring to do violence
To the still night by force of speech.
What do friends need to say that silence
Will not say better? As they reach
The house, they hear Paul's high-pitched piping.
He sits at Phil's typewriter, typing
Jackdaws love my big sphinx of quartz,
While Schwarz, who's feeling out of sorts,
Yawns redly. Paul now sees them, utters
A war whoop and insists that Ed
Play chess. When Paul's been put to bed,
As Ed prepares to leave, Phil mutters,
"Ed, stay tonight. Sue's got guests. Please?"
He smiles at Ed, and Ed agrees.

5.41   Next morning in the St. Ann Chapel
Ed sinks into the Latin mass.
Although he does his best to grapple
With the degenerate morass
Where his sick soul is doomed and drifting,
He finds the plainsong too uplifting
To concentrate (to his chagrin)
On unoriginal thoughts of sin.
Confession helps to ease the pricking
Of his relentless conscience. Ed
Now rejoins Phil. The deep wine-red
Blood of the olives they were picking
Has left on the white tub a stain,
Dark, inerasable, profane.

5.42   Instructions come from Mrs. Craven
       With quartermasterly aplomb,
       The piercing vision of a raven,
       The animation of a bomb:
       "Drain out the bathtub, Paul—Ed, weigh out
       A pound of salt—Rowena, lay out
       Dry towels on the table—Joan,
       Twelve lemons from that tree! ... I'll phone
       Some restaurants for their empty pickle
       And mustard jars.... Matt, olive oil!—
       Rinse the fruit once more, Chuck—Phil, boil
       The water—Sure, I'll pay a nickel
       For every jar. (They're worth two bucks
       Apiece!) Now, turmeric's the crux...."

5.43   The salt's mixed as the water's heated.
       An egg's released upon the brine.
       It floats! The first stage is completed.
       Phase two: In stratified design,
       Bands of plump olives and thick slices
       Of lemon, dusted well with spices,
       Are laid inside each pickling jar.
       Now into each packed reservoir
       A sluice of cooling brine is pouring.
       A seal of olive oil to spare
       The olives from the ambient air—
       And the jar's set aside for storing.
       The lid's screwed tightly; sighs are heaved;
       The label's stuck: the task's achieved!

5.44   The sixteen jars are now divided
       Among the workers, two jars each.
       By now it's evening. Ed's decided
       He must drive back—unto the breach
       Once more, once more back to the city,
       To Monday's mundane nitty-gritty
       Of nine to five. He hears Phil say,
       "You're a real hit with Paul. Look, stay
       Another night, Ed. In the morning
       Before the rush hour, you can go.
       As for my feelings, well...." And so
       Ed stays on and, as day is dawning
       Across Phil's double bed next day,
       Packs bag and beast, and drives away.

Six

6.1   How beautiful it is, when waking,
       To find one's lover at one's side;
       The delicate slow light is breaking
       Irresolutely through the wide
       Bay windows of their bedroom, falling
       On Liz's hair, and John's recalling
       How last night she untied it, how
       It flowed between his hands; but now
       She lies asleep, unswiftly breathing;
       Her thoughts are not with him, her dreams
       Traverse the solitary streams
       Of inward lands, yet her hair, wreathing
       The pillow in a mesh of light,
       Returns to him the fugitive night.

6.2   Or after earnest hours of earning
(Surveys to check, reports to file),
How wonderful it is, returning
To the retreat of a friend's smile
And a shared meal; to know, if only
For this one night, one won't be lonely;
That the obtrusion of the day
—Its grit and strain—will wear away.
This story's time lens is retreating—
Not with intention to confuse
But rather to update the news:
It is two months since their first meeting.
Liz has invited John tonight
To dine with her by candlelight.

6.3   Over a lenten supper (Liz's
New diet, chiefly celery
And bean curd) conversation fizzes
With its old liveliness: their spree
Of baby babble, if belated
In its morendo, has abated,
And some of what in speech and trait
It served to mask or mitigate—
John's acid bolts of irritation
Once inoffensively concealed
In swathing gurgles—lie revealed;
Or Liz's soft infatuation
With the gestalt group she attends.
But, for all this, the two stay friends.

6.4 Prone to excessive sugar-eating,
   Liz vows to cut it down this year.
   She finds each week's gestalt group meeting
   Sustains her will to persevere.
   A regulated distribution
   Of contraband's the best solution—
   Not total abstinence, but, say,
   A spoon or two (or three) a day
   (Liqueur but not dessert exempted).
   Such is the regimen she's sworn.
   The temperate schedule that she's drawn
   To curb desire is first attempted
   One Saturday when John's away.
   By ten her nerves begin to fray.

6.5 By noontime, sugar-crazed and restive,
   Her will deserts her. She would give
   Up Charlemagne for one digestive,
   No, half a gingersnap. Why live
   If life is pain and deprivation?
   Untimely ripped of sweet sensation
   Her taste buds salivate in vain.
   And now the aura of migraine
   Lays siege around her field of vision.
   Darkness descends upon her eyes.
   With ice bags round her head she lies—
   Imagining (with shocked precision)
   Her body suddenly immense
   With carbohydrate corpulence.

6.6   While Liz "reactivates holistic
      Modes of ingestion," John, although
      Intrinsically antagonistic
      To est, gestalt, the whole trousseau
      Of answers "ready-made but flaky"
      (To use his words), maintains a shaky
      Rein on his tongue, but can't resist,
      Occasionally, a baiting twist:
      "Liz, unimpulsive, square, and prudent,
      Before you wholly waste away,
      Inform your suppliant, I pray,
      Of what new fad are you the student?"
      When John is in this kind of mood
      Liz threatens she'll boycott all food.

6.7   They go to the ballet together,
      See movies once or twice a week,
      Take walks; the February weather
      Lures the quince blossoms to a peak
      Of pinkness on the leafless hedges.
      Mimosas bloom, and springtime edges
      Into the city fragrantly.
      Another month, and now we see
      Them poring over want ads, searching
      The dossiers of real estate
      Agents.... Eureka! A sedate
      Queen Anne Victorian is perching
      —Capacious and heaven-sent—
      High on a hill, first floor for rent.

6.8   Despite its turret and its shingles,
Its size lends it a sober air.
Its architecture deftly mingles
Three styles with ecumenic flair—
A cuvée equable yet zestful.
It's true, the wallpaper's unrestful:
The previous occupant, inspired
By zeal for innovation, hired
Two out-of-work avant-garde artists
Who set to work obediently
But in short order proved to be
Ungovernable à-la-cartists;
With drools of chocolate, olive green,
And salmon pink they smeared the scene.

6.9   But, as Liz says, it has potential.
Their evenings and their weekends they
Now spend on stripping the sequential
Layers of mismatched paint away.
Now they've retrieved the handsome molding.
John waves his knife with joy, beholding
The petals of a grand rosette
No longer choked and overset
With plaster on the reborn ceiling.
Now, lost in a creative dream,
He rollers triple coats of cream
Upon the walls; and Liz is kneeling
With rag and polish to restore
The luster of the hardwood floor.

6.10   Fluorescent fixtures are abolished
And mellower lamps placed in their stead;
The wide bay windows, washed and polished,
Pour spendthrift sunlight on the bed.
Liz measures rugs, and John displaces
Chic cabinets with old bookcases,
Soft sofas in beige corduroy
And (so that Charlemagne won't deploy
His claws on drapes) a post for scratching.
Once they have moved in, they invite
Their whole acquaintance to the rite
Of housewarming. But since we're catching
Up with events described above,
We'll shun redundancy and move

6.11   Directly to the morning after.
The sun shines brightly in. The birds'
Aubade replaces last night's laughter,
Professor Pratt's impassioned words,
The broken glasses, the emetic
Sheep music, even the splenetic
Yowls of the vengeful Charlemagne;
And all is quiet once again.
Slack, honey-humming weekend morning,
Sweet sanctuary from a world
In which we're whipped and whisked and whirled!
John sloths in bed awhile, then, yawning,
Attends to coffee. Liz sleeps on,
Though once or twice she murmurs, "John."

6.12   John reads the *San Francisco Chronicle*,
        Sipping his dark Colombian brew.
        He chuckles over an ironical
        Column by Hoppe, turns to view
        The visceral grouches of the crabby
        Herman curmudgeon, scans Dear Abby,
        Miss Manners' prim, refreshing views
        On etiquette, and then the news—
        Which tells no more than the survival
        Of greed and fear and pain and hate.
        John sighs, and thinks of Liz, and Fate,
        Warmed by the solace of arrival:
        A loner who at last has come,
        In a new house, to a new home.

6.13   John looks about him with enjoyment.
        What a man needs, he thinks, is health;
        Well-paid, congenial employment;
        A house; a modicum of wealth;
        Some sunlight; coffee and the papers;
        Artichoke hearts adorned with capers;
        A Burberry trench coat; a Peugeot;
        And in the evening, some Rameau
        Or Couperin; a home-cooked dinner;
        A Stilton, and a little port;
        And so to a duvet. In short,
        In life's brief game to be a winner
        A man must have.... oh yes, above
        All else, of course, someone to love.

6.14   Ah, John, don't take it all for granted.
Perhaps you think Liz loves you best.
The snooker table has been slanted.
A cuckoo's bomb lies in the nest.
Be warned. Be warned. Just as in poker
The wildness of that card, the joker,
Disturbs the best-laid plans of men,
So too it happens, now and then,
That a furred beast with feral features
(Little imagined in the days
When, cute and twee, the kitten plays),
Of that familiar brood of creatures
The world denominates a cat,
Enters the game, and knocks it flat.

6.15   Let me recant. Did I say enter?
Indeed, he was already there,
The *ab initio* resenter
Of the whole pastel-tinged affair—
The grizzled cat, grim and disdainful
Of human weakness, lets his painful
Love of his mistress-heroine
(Who saved his life once) shrive her sin;
But as for John, the old tom tabby
Scratches his proffered hand of truce.
No tribute lamb chops can seduce
Him from his hate. His coat, grown shabby,
Conceals an ever-green-tongued flame
Of jealousy time cannot tame.

6.16   Why scratch a scratching post when trousers
Present themselves? Why bite a bone?
Why hunt mere mice like lesser mousers
When, having gnawed the telephone
Receiver when you sensed the presage
Of an impending urgent message
From John's curt boss, who can't afford
To waste time, you can short the cord?
Why vex yourself with paltry matters
When a report named *Bipartite
Para-Models of Missile Flight*
Can casually be torn to tatters?
And why, in short, crave vapid food
When you can drink your foe's heart's blood?

6.17   Blood! This is no farfetched analogy.
In this connection it's germane
To note his psychic genealogy:
The warrior blood of Charlemagne
Brims with—a bonus for a rhymer—
The hunting spirit of Selima,
The wits of Fritz, the fierce élan
Of the exultant Pangur Bán.
The grand Tiberian Atossa
And the electric Cat Jeoffry
Are honored in a pedigree
Long as your arm and high as Ossa.
I list these but to illustrate
The hybrid vigor of the great.

6.18   How does John dare, the loathed intruder,
        To breach the bounds of his domain,
        Usurp his realm, or, to be cruder,
        To rape his solitary reign—
        Inviolate since when, as a kitten
        —Lost, ear-torn orphan—he had smitten
        Liz's soft schoolgirl heart with love?
        How dare John think—Great Cats above!—
        Cohabitation spells immunity?
        That sordid catnip could replace
        His mistress's nightly embrace?
        And how, with cavalier impunity
        Dare *he* share Liz's bed and, more,
        Lock Charlemagne outside the door?

6.19   Is it then come full circle for you,
        Old Cat, old friend, who pawed the door
        Of a strange house till Lizzie saw you,
        So many swift-spent years before?
        Is it surprising that that kitten,
        Famished and fearful, should have bitten
        Her arm with hunger and relief,
        Or proved half watchman and half thief?
        To supplement his ample ration
        Liz gave him sips of chardonnay.
        (Not a wise habit, by the way.)
        He loved her with a loyal passion
        And showered her with vineyard mice,
        Truly, a homage without price.

6.20   Year followed year. Liz followed knowledge,
Then a career; and Charlemagne
First followed game, then Liz to college,
As faithful (though not as inane)
As Mary's lamb or bumbling bassets.
Blessed with the atavistic assets
Of pride and deep-throated delight
In freedom, what was his by right
—His time's use—he, in willing deference,
Whenever Liz was sad or bored,
Gave to the mistress he adored.
One hand upon a work of reference,
One on his gray and orange fur,
She stroked him, while he purred to her.

6.21   What did that purr reflect? The tender
Fealty of a one-person cat?
Or memories of nights of splendor
When with a snarling caveat
The territorial marauder
Scattered his rivals in disorder
To quench some she-cat's arching wiles
Upon the clattering star-lit tiles?
Or, as he aged, the sweet security
Of love that mellows in old casks
Whose ebbing essence molds and masks
The vintage of its youthful purity?—
Old Cat, who with the injured roar
Of lions, once more paws the door!

6.22   "O Charlemagne, thou little knowest
The mischief done." John stares at his
Defunct report. "That was the lowest
Blow that you could have struck." And Liz,
Distressed in almost equal measure
At her cat's glee and John's displeasure,
Reproaches Charlemagne in slow
And serious terms. "... But John, I know
It's just a temporary reaction—
House-moving has disturbed his poise,
And then that party and that noise...,"
While Charlemagne with satisfaction
Enters the bedroom calmly, sits
On the duvet and warms his wits.

6.23   That night Liz works late. John retires.
She scans tracts on insurance law,
On Acts of God and covered fires.
With twitching hands and quivering jaw
John, naked, bursts into the study.
"Jesus Christ! Liz—your fucking buddy—
That hellish—God!—I'll kill the beast!"
"John ... John, calm down, calm down, at least
Tell me what happened. Did you tease him?"
"Me tease him? That freak climbed the bed
And urinated near my head.
Enough's enough! Liz, don't appease him.
Have that cat neutered. It'll cure
All his aggressions, that's for sure."

6.24 When John's invective grows too torrid
   ("I'll cut them off myself," et al.),
   Liz exclaims, "John, don't be so horrid."
   "Well, ship him off to Senegal
   Or somewhere—Liz, you'd better do it—
   Or—mark my words—that cat will rue it."
   "Oh, darling, don't be so annoyed."
   "What should I be then? Overjoyed?"
   "Of course not, dear. I'm very sorry.
   Let's change the sheets. He's twelve years old.
   He really has a heart of gold."
   "I'll bet!" "Well, dear, try not to worry.
   As for that other thing, that would
   —At his age—do more harm than good."

6.25 "So what should I do—grin and bear it?"
   "Make sure the bedroom door is locked!"
   That night Charlemagne tries to tear it
   Down, but defeated, head half cocked
   In caution and in concentration,
   Turns his mature consideration
   To where John's briefcase, custom-made
   In Polish pigskin, has been laid,
   Open, at John's desk in the study—
   And, using more of skill than force,
   Deals with the matter in due course:
   A disembowelment unbloody
   But satisfactorily complete:
   Reprisal sudden, stern, and meet.

6.26   Next morning comes John's ultimatum,
Not frenzied so much as resigned.
"Some people like cats, and some hate 'em.
I must be of the second kind.
Excuse me if I'm sounding bitter.
I did my best to like this critter,
But, Liz, it takes two—and your cat
Just loathes my innards—and that's that.
He isn't woolly-brained or witless.
Today my briefcase is his prize.
Tomorrow he'll gouge out my eyes.
Believe me, Liz, it scares me shitless.
Either you get that cat declawed
Or I'll—so help me—have 'em sawed

6.27   Right off!" "No! No!" "What are you fearful
Of—for Christ's sake—they're only nails!"
But as he looks into her tearful
Horrified gaze his heart prevails.
She sits there still, without replying.
John says, "Liz . . . Lizzie, please stop crying.
Darling, I'm sorry I upset—"
"They're not! They're not! Ask any vet,"
Liz bursts out, reaching for a tissue,
"Ask Janet—and you'll know you're wrong."
John offers peace, but it's not long
Before he's prompted to reissue
His threat; and Janet is the moot
Court judge brought in to try the suit.

6.28   She sits, on each side an assessor—
       More whimsical than wise, and known
       As Cuff the Great and Link the Lesser.
       "As of this point in time" they've shown
       A lamentable fluctuation
       In judicative concentration
       Beyond a close search of the scene
       Of the alleged crimes. They have been
       Into the bedroom. It has pleased them
       To test the duvet with more pains
       Than justify the likely gains,
       And extra-legal force has eased them
       Into the yard, where they've amused
       Themselves, consorting with the accused.

6.29   There Charlemagne with calm urbanity
       Points out the well-scratched peppertree.
       Avuncular, the soul of sanity,
       With not a quark of jealousy,
       He takes them wandering through the garden
       Digging for gopher burrows. Pardon
       This brief excursus; in the court
       Where an injunction's being sought
       Against John's threatened operation,
       The judgment has come in. Jan says:
       "You're right, Liz. There are other ways.
       Declawing is a mutilation;
       A clawless cat grows far more tense
       And takes to biting for offense.

6.30   However, Liz, you've got to take him
To see a cat psychiatrist.
I know a good one, and she'll make him—
No, don't look stunned—such things exist!
I should explain this. My apologies!
Well, cats, like humans, have psychologies,
And so...." John bursts out: "Jan, you're nuts!"
"But if a cat—" "No ifs and buts!
This whole damn place is going bonkers—
Liz's gestalt, now a cat shrink.
Before I'm pickled in this sink
I'm catching the next flight for Yonkers.
Ciao, California! Land of nuts,
Fruits, vegetables—and their cats and mutts."

6.31   Liz adds, "Jan, it's a poor suggestion.
Charlemagne's a well-balanced cat.
His disposition's not in question."
"I wouldn't put it quite like that—"
Says John with some heat, "well, Jan, maybe...."
Liz says, "John, Charlemagne's no baby.
He won't leap through those hoops. Just let
Him simmer down with time." "Your pet,"
John growls, "is a lopsided menace.
You have a choice. Either agree
To Jan's shrink, or depend on me
To string his reverend guts for tennis
Rackets and violins instead.
That should appeal to Sue and Ed!"

6.32   Liz knuckles under; and John snappily
       Changes the subject. "Well, Jan, how's
       The Sheepfold faring? Pretty happily?
       Why, just last Sunday, as we browsed
       In ShipRecs Liz spied your creation.
       The album cover's a sensation."
       "Well, did you like what it contained?"
       "You know, Jan, I'm so addle-brained . . .
       (John stares intently at his fingers)
       . . . When listening to post-Beatles stuff. . . .
       It must be good, though. . . ." "That's enough!"
       Jan groans. All three laugh. Jan's smile lingers:
       "Well, did you buy it, treacle bun—
       Or count on me to give you one?

6.33   Yes, you lack faith; no, you're a miser!"
       Liz says, "We bought one, Jan." "Oh, good!
       I'll write *For Johnny and Eliza:*
       Co-patrons of my livelihood."
       "I'd put it," John says, "more concisely.
       John. Liz. Love. Jan. will do quite nicely."
       Jan signs, and Liz goes on to ask
       About her latest sculptural task.
       "Well, at the moment, Tutankhamen
       On a raft, spearing—in midstream—
       The God of Evil: that's my theme."
       "I hope it goes well." Jan says, "Amen!"
       Ingests the rest of her Pernod
       And drives back to the studio.

6.34   Charlemagne's sent to Psycho-Kitty
Three times a week, and time goes by.
September gilds the bustling city
Once more, and autumn's lullaby,
Weaving through chatter and commotion,
Sounds dreamily from bay to ocean.
The world, for all its grief and grame,
Goes onward very much the same.
The fog thins out; the rain increases.
With less than customary zest
Jan sits in the Café Trieste
And meditates upon the pieces
Of her fragmented life and art.
" 'The thing is, never to lose heart.'

6.35   Grandma's old dictum's too simplistic
Of course, but what's my A to Z?
'Go with the flow'—that nihilistic
Invertebrate philosophy?
What happens when the flow stops flowing?
Do I give in or keep on going?
My love life's damned. My art is stuck.
I drink too much. My music's muck.
I'd better stop this maudlin listing
Or it'll draw me to the brink
Of—well, I guess that Cuff and Link
Confirm my reason for existing.
Oh yes, and friends. Why don't I call
John for a spiritual overhaul?"

6.36   "Hello. John here.... Oh, hello, Janet....
Yes—no, I wasn't working late.
What? ... Nope, it's Phil who wants to ban it.
Like you, I'm paid, Jan, to create! ...
Hey, Jan, don't blow up for no reason.
That was a joke.... What? Out of season?
All right, it's been withdrawn in haste.
I guess it was in dubious taste.
But Jan, you're really a virago!" ...
Across Jan's face a veil of pain
Passes, but soon she laughs again,
As if there were a fine embargo
Against such words as, without leave,
Enter her heart, and make it grieve.

6.37   "... Tomorrow? Sorry, Jan; I'm busy:
Phil; then a tennis match with Ed....
Next week's not too good ... I and Lizzie ...
Say what, I'll call you back instead."
Jan puts the phone down in dejection
While with remedial affection
The quipster-quadrupeds appear
To climb her knee and lick her ear.
"Not now," says Jan. She sits there, thinking,
While the clock ticks, and minutes pass,
Watching a cube melt in her glass.
The cats are still; they sit there, blinking,
Till summoned: "Octopuss, come here."
Cuff butts her chin; Link tastes a tear.

6.38   Next day is Sunday. In the morning
Phil drops in to see John and Liz:
"Sorry—it seems I can't stop yawning. . . ."
John laughs: "I'd say the reason is
Ecstatic sex from dusk to sunrise."
"Your wit, John, wouldn't make a bun rise."
"Bet I'm right, though." "That's as may be."
"Who is she, Phil?" "Well, wait and see."
"It's not like you to be mysterious
With your old buddies, Philip Weiss."
"Later, John—Liz, I need advice
—No joking, please—this thing is serious—
About the Lungless March this week."
"*That* thing," John mutters with some pique.

6.39   "I thought this was a social visit."
"It is, John. I just thought I'd ask
Liz if—" John breaks in: "Well, Phil, is it
Or isn't it?" A troubled mask
Slips over Phil's face. Liz says, puzzled,
"Free speech among friends can't be muzzled.
Out with it, Phil—what's on your mind?
Let's leave formality behind."
"My question is," says Phil, "can going
Limp when arrested be construed
To be resisting?" "That's a shrewd
Query," Liz murmurs: "True, you're slowing
The process, but they couldn't claim. . . .
Still, I'd go quietly all the same.

6.40 The cops have quite a bit of latitude.
   They could at least make out a case.
   A lot depends upon your attitude...."
   "I think this whole thing's a disgrace,"
   John bursts out, "*and* undemocratic."
   "Right on, John!" Phil says with emphatic,
   Surprised assent. Taken aback,
   John says, "No, I meant *your* attack
   Upon the lab, not what they're doing!
   You've got the courts. You've got the press.
   You've got the vote. To use duress
   Is inexcusable. You're screwing
   Your country while you claim to be
   The high priests of humanity."

6.41 "Look, John, we've talked this out already."
   "If that spitfire phenomenon,
   That spout of gas, hot and unsteady,
   Could be called talk, we may have done.
   As I remember, you waxed lyrical,
   But when it came to an empirical
   Hardheaded look at the real world,
   I found that you had gone and curled
   Up in a corner, drunk and driveling
   About iguanas or some such
   Garbage. We didn't talk too much
   That night, and I can see you swiveling
   Out of my aim again today."
   John's words draw blood; Phil turns at bay.

6.42 "All right, John, if you want discussion,
   Get on with it: we've got free speech."
   "Well, for a start, if you were Russian,
   That wouldn't come so glibly. Each
   Artist or writer there, each poet
   Who's seen the truth and tried to show it
   To his compatriots has been banned,
   Starved, or reviled in his own land—
   Or worse—I doubt I need to tell you
   About the fate of Mandelstam.
   Spout here: you'll come to little harm.
   Spout there: the KGB will sell you
   A ticket to a dexterous shrink
   Who'll drug you dumb to help you think.

6.43 I'll bet a month of psychological
   Incarceration wilts your wit;
   That soon, instead of demagogical
   Heresy you'll howl holy writ.
   Big Bishop knows what's proper for you,
   Expels you if he can't ignore you,
   Infects his pliant flock with spies
   And bloats his paper—*Truth*—with lies.
   Try demonstrating there: publicity
   Will cost more. Drop your job there: wait
   For the swift bear hug of the state. . . .
   But if you credit their duplicity,
   Go bow before the monolith—
   Give them the rope to hang us with."

6.44   John stops, face dark with agitation.
        Phil, startled by his vehemence,
        Starts flashing fire, but moderation
        Prevails: "John, all you've said makes sense—
        Except that I'm not an apologist
        For that regime or that psychologist.
        I'm an American, and I'm glad.
        But their state wouldn't look so bad
        To someone sunk in unemployment
        —Of which we've plenty—or disease.
        Bankrupted by his medical fees
        I doubt that he'd get much enjoyment
        From all his fabled freedoms, or
        Could let his daughter study law.

6.45   I'll even add that their despotic
        Religiosity for Marx
        Acts like—to quote him—a narcotic,
        While privileged ecclesiarchs
        Grow fat on *blat*, cut queues and corners,
        And like battalions of Jack Horners
        Extract plump plums from the joint pie;
        And that they gag, harass, and spy
        On anyone who thwarts the party;
        And hire hacks; but if our forte
        Is that we're free, and don't support
        Our own soft choir of castrati,
        We support those who've given birth
        To the one race-reich left on earth.

6.46   But why did we get into all this?
I know—you said . . . but never mind.
As for the apocalypse: I'd call this
Not theirs or ours. Humankind
Extends beyond our grim theocracies
Or constitutional plutocracies.
This world of ours, this atmosphere
All of us breathe . . . (Phil pauses here
And laughs) . . . I see why you accuse me
Of waxing lyrical. . . . Anyway,
How can you think of we or they
When we're both in the soup? Refuse me
Support, that's fine; but, John, don't doubt
I know what I'm going on about. . . .

6.47   . . . I'll leave some literature here for you.
I don't mean to evangelize.
For all I know the stuff will bore you.
But try to see it through our eyes. . . ."
At this, Phil leaves with John (who, calmer,
Has slowly loosed his cancroid armor)
The Fate of the Earth—a tract by Schell—
And two by Caldicott, as well
As several slim brochures describing
This Friday's march upon that place,
That heartland of the missile race
Named Lungless. Finally, imbibing
A reconciliatory hit
Of dope, Phil murmurs, "Got to split."

6.48 "Phil, wait a second, here's a present
   For Paul: an abalone shell."
   "Thanks, John," Phil smiles, and with a pleasant
   Handshake—a kiss for Liz as well—
   And a brief nod at Dr. Spooner
   ("I piked your lot") drives off. No sooner
   Has John breathed thanks that he's survived
   Phil's phalanxes, than Ed's arrived.
   Liz hugs her brother: "Hello, handsome,
   Why aren't you dressed for tennis?" Ed
   Wryly exclaims, "Makes me see red!
   We've got this big campaign on, and some
   Dodo's just left us in the lurch
   —I've just had time to go to church—

6.49 He left on Thursday, with no warning—
   So we're all working overtime.
   Well, that's the news this Sunday morning!
   I'm sorry, John . . . Liz, that's why I'm
   All suited—but I must be going!"
   Liz smiles at Ed; then, startled, showing
   Signs first of shock, then bafflement,
   Thinks, "Surely there's some accident. . . .
   How can . . . and yet, what other meaning. . . ?"
   And even after Ed has gone
   Seems so preoccupied that John
   Asks, "What's the matter, Liz?" But leaning
   Cheek on hand, Liz, abstracted, stares
   Out of the window, unawares.

Seven

7.1   When fear grows too intense to handle,
We shrink into a private smile,
Surprised when here and there a candle
Drives back the dark a little while,
A little space, before it gutters;
Or in the madness a voice utters
Words full of calm that to us seem
To bear the dry light of a dream
And stain our waking with more sorrow.
The night of hate that covers earth,
The generous country of our birth,
The single land from which we borrow
All that is ours—air, insight, tears,
Our fragile lives—for a few years,

7.2   That night of hate grows dense around us.
We laugh through what we can't dispel,
While apathy and terror hound us
On well-intentioned paths to hell.
Best to concede, to the septic chorus
Of the world's counsels, what's good for us,
And let them, if they choose to, mar
Our common earth with civil war.
Live day to day; relieve a little
What sorrow lies within our scope;
A moratorium on hope
Will, if it makes our laughter brittle,
Lend peace until that day of wrath
When the smooth doomtoys hurtle forth.

7.3   What, after all, is earth's creation?
A virus in the morgue of space.
What's Mozart but a weird vibration
Congenial to a brain-sick race
Rabid with virulence. Why bother
If things like these should maul each other
And, dying, yelp that they have won?
If clouds of dust occlude their sun
From them, it still shines undiminished
In its small galaxy. No change
Of note is likely when this strange
Irradiated beast has finished
Vomiting filth upon its bed
Of inhumanity, and is dead.

7.4 Some disagree. Heroic, silly
   —Whichever—they have gathered here
   In the pre-dawn, dew-damp and chilly,
   On one or two days in the year
   When light and night share day's dimension
   In equal halves. To ease their tension
   (For near them, where a cyclone fence
   Delimits the circumference
   Of Lungless Labs, police stand sentry,
   Guarding a road, checkpost, and gate),
   They sing aloud, and celebrate
   Fall's somber equinoctial entry
   By lighting candles in an arc
   Against the encroachment of the dark.

7.5 Dawn rises over Lungless redly.
   The pioneers of the blockade
   Are joined now by a motley medley;
   A marching carnival parade
   Starts out from Lungless Park, cavorting
   Along to Lungless Labs, supporting
   Those who risk prison to defy
   The weaponry they all decry.
   Young couples, schoolchildren, grandmothers,
   Old hippies, punks with hair dyed green,
   Staid-suited men who've never seen
   Another demonstration, others
   Who've been to scores, walk hand in hand
   Toward the place where death is planned.

7.6   Those who devise these weapons—decent,
Adjusted, family-minded folk—
Don't think they plan death. Their most recent
Bomb (which, as an engaging joke,
They dubbed "the cookie cutter") batters
Live cells and yet—this is what matters—
Leaves buildings and machines intact—
This butchering brainspawn is in fact
Soothingly styled a "radiation
Enhancement device" by these same men.
Blind in their antiseptic den
To the obscene abomination
Of the refined ampoules of hate
Their ingenuity helps create,

7.7   They go to work, attend a meeting,
Write an equation, have a beer,
Hail colleagues with a cheerful greeting,
Are conscientious, sane, sincere,
Rational, able, and fastidious.
Through hardened casings no invidious
Tapeworm of doubt, no guilt, no qualm
Pierces to sabotage their calm.
When something's technically attractive,
You follow the conception through,
That's all. What if you leave a slew
Of living dead, of radioactive
"Collateral damage" in its wake?
It's just a job, for heaven's sake.

7.8　They breed their bombs here; others aim them
　　　　—Young targeteers at their controls—
　　　　At living souls, to kill and maim them
　　　　(Although their unemotive goals
　　　　Talk not of "death" but "optimizing
　　　　Effective yield"), while, mobilizing
　　　　Uncertain radar, we explore
　　　　The skies and prod ourselves to war.
　　　　Then, locked inside their lethal closet,
　　　　Go codes received, launch keys in place,
　　　　Bright crew-cut zombies will efface
　　　　All humankind. Too late to posit
　　　　What made them fire from the hip.
　　　　A flight of geese? A faulty chip?

7.9　Fatigues, down jackets, and bandannas,
　　　　Handicapped veterans in wheelchairs,
　　　　American flags and rainbow banners,
　　　　A band for Sousa, priests for prayers,
　　　　A replica of the grim reaper,
　　　　Placards—"I am my brother's keeper,"
　　　　"Nice folks don't use nukes," "Work for life,
　　　　Not death," and a huge "Strive with strife"—
　　　　Quarreling, waving, wrangling, singing,
　　　　The lively ununanimous throng,
　　　　Two thousand minds, two thousand strong,
　　　　Submerge their disagreements, bringing
　　　　Common concern and hope to bear
　　　　Against the smithy of "hardware."

7.10   Phil hears the crowd from where he's standing,
Engaged in a brisk conference
With two TV reporters. Handing
Out pamphlets labeled *Common Sense*
About Our Common Fate, Phil mentions
Briefly their plans and their intentions:
"We'll have a speech by Father O'Hare;
Then, in small groups, we'll walk out there
And cross that line of demarcation.
While we block traffic going through,
The cops will grab us two by two
—That's standard for a demonstration—
And haul us off to jail—in those
Yellow school buses, I suppose.

7.11   As evidence of our sincerity
We won't resist." The TV crew
Shoot several reels off with celerity,
Thank Phil, and turn to interview
A Lungless Labs spokeswoman: "Really,
These games cost the taxpayer dearly,
And have a minimal effect
Upon the labs. To misdirect
Attack upon an institution
That serves the nation's a perverse,
Quixotic, petulant, or worse,
An un-American resolution.
As every president can attest,
What we do here is for the best."

7.12   Phil looks around him. An inflated
        Blue whale with *Save the Humans* scrawled
        Across its side is inundated
        By clambering children. The so-called
        Elders for Peace are pressing flowers
        On the police. A sergeant glowers,
        "Ma'am, please step back across that line. . . .
        Ma'am, that is no concern of mine. . . .
        No, thank you, ma'am, it's not a marriage."
        Phil chuckles. A new vision nears:
        A woman with a placard steers
        A cat strapped in a baby carriage
        Toward him. "Almost looks like Liz. . . .
        Good heavens . . . surely not!" It is.

7.13   "Liz! Liz!" Phil shouts. "This is fantastic!
        What are you doing here? And John—
        Where's he?" With an enthusiastic
        Bear hug Phil beams a smile down on
        Liz, who, one hand held down, restraining
        Charlemagne (whose great-lunged complaining
        Has risen several decibels)
        And one hand on a sign that spells
        Cats and attorneys are disarming.
        Why aren't we all? gasps out, "Ow! Phil,
        Let go of—Charlemagne, keep still!
        Don't—Ouch! That wasn't very charming!
        Look, you've drawn blood, I hope you're glad.
        Now, Charlemagne, don't make me mad. . . .

7.14 . . . Perhaps I oughtn't to have brought him.
He isn't used to the melee.
It's the jazz band that's overwrought him . . .
But, Phil, as I was going to say,
John isn't here. Did you expect him?"
"Well, no, it's just that I connect him . . ."
"Thanks, Phil!" Liz smiles: "That isn't too
Astute—or flattering—of you.
I too can . . . by the way, how's Eddy?"
"Eddy?" asks Phil, "Oh, Ed—I see.
I don't . . . why are you asking *me*?"
But now the microphones are ready,
Father O'Hare says, "Friends, a word—"
And the brief parley is deferred.

7.15 Bespectacled, short, nervous, chubby,
With few gray hairs for sixty years,
And scruffy cassock, the priest's tubby
And unimposing form appears
A curious temple for the oracle;
And every hint of oratorical
Expectancy is squelched when he,
Bent down on an unsteady knee,
Two fingers fumbling with his collar,
Gathers the notes his jittery hands
Dropped on the ground; but when he stands
And starts to speak, the pudgy scholar
(By nature; activist by choice)
Holds them with his soft resonant voice.

7.16   Now both blockaders and supporters
Are silent as the priest says, "Friends,
Sisters and brothers, sons and daughters,
The little time each of us spends . . .
Can everyone at the back hear me?
Yes? Excellent—and all those near me—
Not too loud? . . . Well, these few short years
We spend pursuing our careers,
Our needs, our longings, our obsessions
Upon this earth, once gone, are dead.
Of some who've spent their time, it's said
They gathered manifold possessions;
Of some, they broke their lives for wealth;
Of some, their striving broke their health.

7.17   Of some it's said they learned to master
The secret fusion of the sun,
Of some that they ran, rode, swam faster
Than till their advent man had done,
Of some, they eked life out as drudges,
Of some—but any way one judges
Their lives or ours, to dole out blame
Or praise, one attribute may claim
To cut across all our partitions
Of wealth and vigor, fame and wit:
Did they serve life? Or injure it?
These are more naked oppositions
Than can sieve truth in every case,
But we may use them when we face

7.18   Choices such as, today, we're facing.
       What is our will in life? To race
       As, lemming-like, mankind is racing
       To liquidation, or to face
       With what small strength we have, the massive
       Machine of omnicide, impassive,
       Oiled by inertia and by hate
       And the smooth silver of the state?
       Today we meet in celebration
       Of life; some have their children here;
       And all of us are of good cheer.
       Indeed, with our incarceration
       In those yellow school buses, we
       May find ourselves compelled to be

7.19   As little children. Let's inquire
       With the same childishness as they,
       Should we not try to douse a fire
       That threatens to consume away
       Not just our home but the whole city?
       Or with a worldly-wise and witty
       Shrug and rejoinder should we turn
       The volume up and let Rome burn?
       Well, we have gathered here this morning
       In disparate but harmonious voice
       To show that we have made our choice;
       That we have hearkened to the warning
       That hate and fear kill; and are here
       Confronting death and hate and fear.

7.20   Hate is a subtle weed; vagaries
        Of soil and time give it new growth.
        Only the food of hatred varies;
        England and Germany were both
        Our bitterest enemies; we hated
        Each of them. Yet when we had sated
        Our enmity and made them friends,
        Hate found new sustenance for its ends.
        The English gone, it found the Spanish.
        Japan defeated, China served
        To keep its lethal life preserved.
        Its victim crushed, it would not vanish.
        Even before we'd reached Berlin,
        Moscow was our new sump of sin.

7.21   Hate shifts with diplomatic fashion.
        To love is to be resolute.
        By Christ's own sacrifice and passion,
        We cannot flinch, we must not mute
        The strength and grace of his humanity
        By acquiescing in insanity.
        Neither crusading frenzy nor
        The specious pleading of 'just war'
        Permits the least justification
        Of that which, once used, will ensure
        That God's creation won't endure.
        Without hate, without hesitation,
        Taking our freedom in our hand,
        Let us each pledge that here we stand.

7.22   Though Catholic, I make no apology
        For quoting someone we've proclaimed
        The arch-monk of our demonology
        These several hundred years. I aimed
        To show that in this murderous weather
        That threatens, we will stand together,
        As now; and with our common breath
        Cry out against our common death.
        Catholic and Episcopalian,
        Lutheran, Baptist, Methodist,
        Jew, Muslim, Buddhist, atheist,
        We are all here; no one is alien
        Now radiation's common laws
        Impel us into common cause.

7.23   It was once asked on Belsen's ashes,
        'Where were you then? Where was the Church?'
        If once more our high sentence clashes
        With our inaction, we need search
        No further for complicit stigma
        Than those hands bearing the enigma
        Of blood and body in the mass.
        Please God, this will not come to pass.
        Our bishops' recent pastoral letter
        On nuclear arms demands a freeze.
        Today our own archdiocese
        Of San Francisco's an abettor
        —They've lent us transport—in this fight
        Against the law, but for the right.

7.24　I have heard some who denigrate us
　　　Claim that we wish to abrogate
　　　The constitutional hiatus
　　　Between religion and the state.
　　　Our job, they say, is to be godly
　　　While the state goes on acting oddly.
　　　The scripture for their vision is
　　　'Give unto Caesar what is his.'
　　　Let me observe that separation
　　　Of church and state does not exempt
　　　The church from action, may not tempt
　　　The state from all examination
　　　Of conscience, and ought, lastly, not
　　　To serve as partisan buckshot.

7.25　There are occasions when morality
　　　And civil law are in dispute.
　　　Granted its sole officiality,
　　　Civil law is not absolute.
　　　If we accept our obligation
　　　Not to accept annihilation
　　　Or that, in our name, bombs are hurled
　　　At others elsewhere in the world,
　　　The quote above needs its addenda.
　　　Students who gloss a narrow text
　　　Should read the passage that comes next;
　　　It is suggested that we render
　　　Things that are God's to God, as well
　　　As stocking Caesar's citadel.

7.26   What Caesar, battling for democracy,
       Unasked, relinquished his regime?
       What cotton king decried slavocracy?
       What cat forwent its dish of cream?
       If we expect disinterested
       Judgment from Congress, from our vested
       Arms gluttons—from the White House down—
       We're living in cloud-cuckoo-town.
       We cannot wait for legislation.
       There is no shame in following
       Thoreau and Anthony and King,
       The old traditions of a nation
       That once, two hundred years before,
       In its own birth resisted law.

7.27   There is no time, when escalation
       Bloats our stockpiles with overkill,
       When secular proliferation
       Means that a score of nations will
       Soon hatch these eggs, and when with manic
       Slaver we froth the world to panic,
       To nourish niceties. We must pray,
       Reflect, and act in any way
       —Peaceful; that needs no emphasizing—
       That may decelerate, reduce,
       Or ban the inception, test, and use
       Of weaponry so brutalizing
       Its mere birth brings opprobrium down
       Upon the name of Lungless Town.

7.28   Workers of Lungless Labs—when dying
Will you be proud you were midwife
To implements exemplifying
Assault against the heart of life?
You knew their purpose, yet you made them.
If you had scruples, you betrayed them.
What pastoral response acquits
Those who made ovens for Auschwitz?
Indeed, it's said that the banality
Of evil is its greatest shock.
It jokes, it punches its time clock,
Plays with its kids. The triviality
Of slaughtering millions can't impinge
Upon its peace, or make it cringe.

7.29   Killing is dying. This equation
Carries no mystical import.
It is the literal truth. Our nation
Has long believed war was a sport.
Unoccupied, unbombed, undying,
While 'over there' the shells were flying,
How could we know the Russian dread
Of war, the mountains of their dead?
We reveled in acceleration
At every level of the race;
And even now we're face to face
With mutual extermination
We talk as blithely as before
Of 'surgical strikes' and 'limited war.'

7.30   There is no victory, no survival,
And no defense, no place to hide,
No limit, and indeed, no rival
In this exhaustive fratricide.
We'll all fall down. Despite resilient
Airs of omniscience, our brilliant
Leaders, when all is said and done,
Have no solution, no, not one.
With quaint autumnal orthodoxy
They point out that America's best:
The Russians can't, they say, protest.
That only means we must stand proxy
For those who cannot speak, but are
As much opposed as we, to war.

7.31   Ten hostages is terrorism;
A million, and it's strategy.
To ban books is fanaticism;
To threaten in totality
All culture and all civilization,
All humankind and all creation,
This is a task of decorous skill
And needs high statesmanship and will.
It takes a deal of moral clarity
To see that it is right to blitz
Each Russian family to bits
Because their leaders' muscularity
—Quite like our own—on foreign soil
Threatens our vanity or 'our' oil.

7.32   *Quo warranto?* By what authority,
        I ask you in the wounds of Christ,
        Does strength confer superiority
        Over God's earth? What has enticed
        Mere things like us into believing
        The world may be left charred and grieving
        In man-made doom at the behest
        Of patriotic interest?
        It's come that close. A Russian freighter
        —In autumn 1962—
        Halted before the line we drew
        To cut off Cuba. Minutes later,
        And our own manly president would
        Have finished off mankind for good.

7.33   To those who with tall intellectual
        Prudence sniff at our brashness and
        State that our stance is ineffectual,
        That with our puny sling to stand
        Against this latter-day Goliath
        Is not wise, let me ask, 'How dieth
        The wise man? As the fool.' To turn
        Your face from horror will not earn
        You an indulgence. Help us fight it.
        Two hundred years ago, indeed,
        Who would have dreamed slaves would be freed?
        That's one example, and I cite it
        To show how conscience, starting small,
        In God's good time, may conquer all.

7.34   From history we may learn two lessons:
How slowly—and how fast—things change.
Whether the permanent quiescence
Of fear—or life—occurs, it's strange
Not to know how long we'll be striving,
Or which succeeds in first arriving;
But whether we prevail or lose,
One thing is certain: we must choose.
God won't forsake you or ignore you—
So don't forsake him. Let me close
With Deuteronomy's plain prose.
Here it is: 'I have set before you
Life and death . . . therefore choose life.'
Or, as that sign says, 'Strive with strife.' "

7.35   The priest sits quietly down. Applauding,
The crowd now rises to its feet.
Liz nudges Phil: "Well, Phil, according
To your lights—this is in complete
Confidence—did his Bible bluster
Pass your severe Judaic muster?"
Phil smiles, "I ought to tell you, I'm
Renting a rabbi for next time.
But sure, I'm used to it. Remember,
I was once married to a goy.
And even Paul himself, poor boy,
Has been polluted with an ember
Or two of gentile coal in his
Severe Judaic fire. But, Liz,

7.36　　Quit baiting me, and let me bait you.
　　　　How come your masters let you go?
　　　　I don't mean to insinuate you
　　　　Don't have your own views, but, you know,
　　　　Today's a weekday. Cobb & Kearny
　　　　Must miss their golden-haired attorney.
　　　　And doesn't John lament and grieve
　　　　That you've absconded without leave?
　　　　I can't believe that this excursion
　　　　Carries his blessing." "Phil, you're wrong.
　　　　Actually, John expressed his strong
　　　　Approval of our day's diversion.
　　　　His exact words were 'Go to hell—
　　　　And take your fucking cat as well!'

7.37　　I think tonight that I'll appease him
　　　　By treating him to dinner at
　　　　The Tree of Heaven. That should please him. . . .
　　　　Keep in those claws, Magnificat!
　　　　Just one hour more. We'll soon be going
　　　　Back to the car. . . . Phil, when he's showing
　　　　This kind of restlessness, it's best
　　　　To humor him. . . . Will they arrest
　　　　You soon? It looks like they're beginning
　　　　To block the roadway." "Well, not yet.
　　　　The game's just under way. I get
　　　　To enter in the second inning.
　　　　Why don't you get arrested too?"
　　　　"Phil, I'm not as extreme as you."

7.38   "Extreme?" "I mean, I'm not committed
In the same way." "I see." "But, Phil,
If you've got something quarter-witted
That I can do to help, I will.
And Phil . . . I really do admire you."
"Well, Liz, you could—but no—they'd fire you."
"What?" "Well, I thought that legal aid. . . ."
Liz looks downcast: "No, I'm afraid
That's the one thing that I can't proffer.
The firm would squawk . . . but taking care
Of Paul perhaps—could I help there?"
"Well, thanks, Liz, that's a generous offer.
If you could spare an evening, yes,
Please visit him at this address.

7.39   Tell him I'm fine, and will be coming
Home soon; and to be good." By now
The Lungless intersection's humming
With cars, crowds, and police. Somehow
—Now as offender, now as warden—
The monitors maintain a cordon
Across the road. All traffic stops.
With tactical arrests the cops
Disrupt the barrier for a minute.
While the blockade's re-forming, two
Deft cars (work badges checked) get through
The metal fence; and once within it,
Their drivers, irked at having been
Delayed, revert to their routine.

7.40   In choreographed concatenation
       The demonstrators quietly go
       Across the line of demarcation
       And lay themselves down in a row.
       The traffic halts; they are arrested;
       With sharp civility requested
       To walk, and on refusal, dragged
       To the school buses, where they're tagged
       With plastic handcuffs. Once inside them,
       The ex-blockaders, unsubdued,
       Revived by the bright yellow mood
       Of their detention buses, ride them
       Singing "Give Peace a Chance," locked tight
       In a slow transport of delight.

7.41   Now a diversified assortment
       Of persons wedded to the cause
       Appears, whose singular deportment
       Draws larger measures of applause.
       A figure high on stilts approaches
       The roadway at high speed, encroaches
       On the exclusionary zone
       That the police claim as their own,
       But it's not easy to arrest her
       When her arms float four feet above
       Their heads, and her well-trained pet dove
       Sullies their caps. Who dares divest her
       Of her appendages? Who'll bell
       The dove—at risk of his lapel?

7.42   A coffin, fashioned like a missile,
Is shouldered by a dozen friends.
A human pine tree, full and fissile,
Decked in pine branches, greenly wends
Its way into the intersection,
Splits up and joins the insurrection,
While skeleton-suited youths throw flowers
On the windshields of halted cars.
Her grandson's snapshot, square and cheerful,
Pinned to her chest, hair in blue rinse,
A doughty dame tries to convince
An officer, who, almost tearful,
Gasps, lugging her toward a bus:
"Ma'am, this thing isn't up to us."

7.43   Meanwhile, to counterpoint this strenuous
Nonviolence, on the sidelines
A sponsor of the march (ingenuous,
But perspicacious too) assigns
Two-minute slots for public sharing
Of audience response. Declaring,
"The floor is free now. If you'd like
To say a few words, here's the mike,"
He chairs a talk show, "Nuclear Witness."
The TV cameras close in.
A pastor talks on "Crime—or Sin?"
A doctor on "Fallout and Fitness,"
And several others on why they
Decided to protest today.

7.44 When no one grabs the mike, the previous
   Speaker asks someone in the crowd
   To follow him, and by this devious
   Tactic the shyest or most proud
   Invitee's shamed into consenting
   —However fearful or tormenting
   The thought of public speech may be—
   To pool his feelings. Suddenly,
   To Liz's horror, an alarming
   Voice rings out: "You there, with the pram
   And cat—you're speaking next." "I am?"
   "Yes, you, attorney who's disarming."
   Liz says, "I just can't, there's no way—
   Oh, Jesus, Phil, what'll I say?"

7.45 "Anything, Liz—it doesn't matter.
   If you can talk for hours in court..."
   "That's different." "Bullshit. Just don't spatter
   Your speech with jargon." With a snort
   Phil grabs the mike and hands it to her
   While the unflustered interviewer
   Asks her her name: "Now feel at ease
   To speak on anything you please.
   It's just two minutes." At first nervous,
   Liz thaws. She says, "There's something I
   Have often thought of. If we die
   —We humans, that is—it may serve us
   Right for our silliness and hate.
   But what we cannot vindicate

7.46   Is killing all the other fauna
That have developed on the earth.
On field or floe, in every corner,
From Maine to Thule, from Minsk to Perth,
They'll die. I'm not exaggerating.
The reason is illuminating;
Blinding, in fact. With ruined eyes
A cheetah, or an insect, dies
—And lingeringly—of starvation.
Deplete the ozone layer by two
And let more ultraviolet through—
Violà! We've blinded dumb creation—
Although its delegate, my cat,
Would claim he's not as dumb as that.

7.47   Well, we are. It's been calculated
If only half our bombs explode
—Just half, that's all—we'll have created
A quite sufficient overload
Of nitrogen oxides to gobble
Up half our ozone. We may squabble
About percentage points; what's clear
Is that each shrew, each fly, each deer
Who isn't wearing tinted glasses
Will suffer retinal burns, go blind,
And starve, and die. And so, mankind
—That radiant species—when it passes
Will leave the generous bequest
Of death and blindness to the rest."

7.48   Liz stops, and puts the mike down. Twenty
           Seconds pass. No one speaks at all.
           She looks at Phil: "Jargon aplenty,
           But none from law!" A caterwaul
           Reminds the world that dumb creation
           Is happiest in its habitation—
           Or, rather, in its habitat.
           At any rate, Liz strokes her cat,
           Appeasing his dissatisfaction:
           "I'll take you home. Don't cry—I will. . . .
           I must be off now. Good luck, Phil—
           I'd better take corrective action.
           His mood's sunk downwards far too far . . ."
           And wheels him townwards to the car.

Eight

8.1   Evening; Phil's house. "What's the detergent
      That's kept your soul unsoiled this time?
      You've always known the problem's urgent
      But haven't knelt down in the grime
      To help your friends, Ed, by investing
      A few days of your life protesting.
      Do you imagine, if you pray,
      The megatons will wilt away?"
      "No." "Well?" "Well—Phil—it's the mentality
      —Us : them—the last thing that we need—
      That's the first thing these protests breed.
      Self-righteous superficiality
      Won't extirpate the roots of sin
      Or cure us of the mess we're in."

8.2   "And what's your plan for—extirpation?"
"To curb our own complicity
In violence and in exploitation.
We are ourselves the enemy.
This man builds bombs—but am I using
More than my share of goods, abusing
The birthright of my fellows? Do
I dominate them? ..." "Ed, that's true
—Why even bother to deny it—
But as a practical recourse
Your mea culpa lacks all force.
It's far too slow. I just can't buy it.
By the time your catholicon
Acts on our guts, we'll all be gone.

8.3   ... Oh, by the way, have you met feisty
Father O'Hare?" "No, what's he like?"
"Brimstone cum brains, I'd say, and Christ—he
Knows how to wield a wicked mike;
And more, to act on what he preaches."
Ed smiles: "I read one of his speeches
Last week—*Priest Blasts Nukes.*" "Yes, that's how
The press reported it. Well, now,
You two should meet, Ed. He's compelling.
It may do you some good to find
A man of God who doesn't mind
The temporal dunghill. There's no telling
What the impromptu thunderstroke
Of his discourses might provoke.

8.4 But I don't mean to preach. The tension
   Of the last week. . . ." Ed says, "I know.
   I'm glad I'm not the first to mention
   Prison; but, well, how did things go?
   Are you all right?" "Oh, sure! They held us
   In circus tents, which served to weld us
   Into coherent troupes of clowns. . . .
   I guess it had its ups and downs."
   "Why tents?" Phil laughs: "We were too numerous
   To fit in Lungless County Jail."
   "The food, Phil?" "Neither cakes and ale
   Nor bread and tears." Phil waxes humorous
   While Ed grills him (with serious mien)
   On their ten days of quarantine.

8.5 The red and green big tops that housed them
   Brought forth a Mardi Gras esprit.
   The sentence they were offered roused them
   To staunch remonstrance. Finally,
   In lieu of a two-year probation
   (Effectively an authorization
   That pawned their First Amendment right
   To go on fighting the good fight),
   The county prosecutors, rattled
   By their refusal to play ball,
   Allowed that time served plus a small
   Fine would suffice. Thus the embattled
   Jailbirds, bedraggled but unclipped,
   Sang their way out to their own script.

8.6   Some of them—a selected sample—
Pleaded not guilty when arraigned
—Among them Phil—as an example
To hearten others who, strength strained,
Had delegated their decrial
Of arms to them. Their jury trial
("Wilfully and maliciously
Obstructing traffic") is to be
Held the next month with high publicity.
"Necessity" is their defense:
A doctrine born of common sense
And common law that waives complicity
When present public hazard proves
The force an impugned act removes.

8.7   As Phil talks on, his eyes grow radiant.
Ed thinks of the first time they met.
The weeks have warped the placid gradient
On which his even wheels were set.
Neither the sense, at every meeting,
Of his heart's full and rapid beating,
Nor the abrupt and scalding rush
Of redness to his face, the flush
When he feels Phil's eyes resting on him,
But something infinite and slow
And tide-like holds his life in tow.
The salt of human love upon him,
To it his leached will yields control,
Whether it stings or heals his soul.

8.8 And yet it seems as if a curtain
   Of doubt has dropped across his eyes.
   "The affairs of men rest still incertain";
   And Ed begins to agonize.
   Is this some mere infatuation
   Fastened to need and admiration?
   Can it survive the abrading years
   Or even till next week? Ed fears
   That in a sense quite fundamental
   He knows Phil less than when they met.
   Phil speaks with openness, and yet
   Refrains from all but accidental
   Reflection on his earlier life,
   His previous loves, his former wife.

8.9 "Phil—" Ed begins with hesitation,
   "Why don't you ever talk of Claire?
   Sometimes, when we're in conversation
   I almost sense that she is there,
   As though your outward eyes were seeing
   Me here before you, but your being
   Imagines her—as if you feel
   It's a betrayal to reveal
   What she was like—it's like a stricture
   Has seized you. I can't visualize
   Even the color of her eyes,
   Her hair. Why don't you have a picture
   Of her—for Paul's sake—anywhere?
   Her name, too—is it Clare or Claire? . . .

8.10   I know I've no rights in this matter.
It's just, somehow, I'd like to know."
Phil laughs, "Ed's trumpet tries to batter
The battlements of Jericho.
Brown. Brown. And with an *i*. Quit bugging
Me, will you, Ed—I'm sick of lugging
This tragic burden week by week.
Some light refreshment—so to speak—
Is what I thirst for. Ed, I love you,
But don't exhume this; there's no sense
In scouring ruins. Why condense
The happiness that floats above you
By seeding it with doubt and pain,
Crystals that force it down as rain?"

8.11   Ed's quiet for a while. Phil's quiet.
Paul's off at the Lamonts' today.
The fridge hums, happy with its diet
Of ice cubes. Clocks click time away,
Contented with its circularity.
Phil yawns. The crackling fissiparity
Of popcorn on the stove returns
Him to the present—and he burns
His thumb endeavoring to extract it.
"You OK? Let me help!" Ed gets
Butter and garlic salt; and sets
Some napkins out. Now they've attacked it
With starved abandon. "Whoa! It's hot
—You're right—but really hits the spot! . . .

8.12   ... Do you like cooking, Phil?" "Not really.
I can't abide its cruelty."
"Cruelty, Phil?" "Right—you don't merely
Pop corns, you beat eggs, wilfully
Stone cherries, whip cream, chop and skewer,
Are happier when cheese is bluer—
And then there's batter, rack of lamb,
And squash, and mace ... ad nauseam.
No. Violence and exploitation
Of co-comestibles would be
A sin. My conscience troubles me
With delicate denunciation:
Far better not to cook, and starve
In purity, than baste and carve."

8.13   Ed frowns. "I wish you'd check your humor.
I sometimes think that you and John
Metastasized from the same tumor.
It's not that it goes on and on
But that there's something cutting to it."
Phil laughs at Ed, "I guess I blew it!
I'm not like John, though. Ed, don't frown....
It's late ... (He yawns) ... Should we walk down
To Printers Inc, and get some coffee?"
"Yes, let's. I need a change of mood.
And, by the way, do they have food?"
"Sure—brownies, muffins, fudge, cake, toffee—
Most of the stuff's so good it hurts—
And all supplied by Just Desserts."

8.14 The enchanted bookstore, vast, rectangular,
   Fluorescent-lit, with Bach piped through
   The glamorous alleys of its angular
   Warren of bookshelves, the dark brew
   Of French roast or Sumatra rousing
   One's weak papillae as one's browsing
   Lead to the famed cups, soon or late,
   That cheer but don't inebriate.
   Magical shoe box! Skilled extractor
   Of my last dime on print or drink,
   Mini-Montmartre, Printers Inc!
   Haven of book freaks, benefactor
   Of haggard hacks like me, who've been
   Quivering for years to your caffeine.

8.15 Replete with coffee and confection,
   Some talk of olives, some of Paul,
   Ed browses through the children's section.
   "*The Wind in the*—no, he's too small—
   And a bit old for Beatrix Potter—
   But *Charlotte's Web* perhaps—that's got a
   Spider as well ... Now for myself...."
   Ed wanders to a sheltered shelf,
   Communes with Ambrose and Augustine,
   And seeks assistance in his search
   For histories of the early church.
   "We don't have much, sir; Bamm is just in...."
   "Something more academic?" "Well,
   That's not the kind of book we sell.

8.16 But we could order it. . . ." Ed, thanking
Him for his pains, moves on to Chess.
He finds Phil leaning on a flanking
Bookshelf, engrossed in *Watercress,*
The Wonder Plant, and How to Grow It.
Ed smiles. Phil says, "Not that you'd know it,
But watercress, I ought to state,
Is one of eight V's in V-8."
Ed laughs: "My dad too likes to dabble
In—he's the meanest trivia nut
In all Sonoma County—but
Talking of eight V's, let's play Scrabble. . . .
D'you have a set?" "Sure. Let's go home
And bicker over *zho* and *clomb.*"

8.17 Back home, to sips of Cherry Heering
("Tastes like cough mixture," ventures Ed),
Phil demonstrates his pluck and daring—
Flamboyant sorties on the red,
Long words impervious to Ed's challenge,
All seven letters used in *phalange*—
While Ed's words, wary, composite,
Short, closed, pointworthy, bit by bit
Chew up the board in ruthless nibbles,
Sealing Phil's options one by one;
And when at last the game is done
And Phil (stuck with a beached Q) scribbles
The final score, Ed smiles in glee
At Phil (who smiles, but ruefully).

8.18   "Let's see that score ... (Ed's eye alights on
A previous game) ... Hey, Phil, who's R?"
"Rowena." "Oh." "Tough player—fights on
Even when obviously too far
Behind to stand a chance of winning.
And even though at the beginning
I'd cream her, since she's had a go
At Russian, monsters like *zemstvo*
Have scored her a few touchdowns." "Do you
See much of her?" "Oh, now and then.
She has a thing for single men—
As you know, Ed." "I never knew you
Thought of yourself as single." "Well,
Single, divorced—it's hard to tell. . . .

8.19   . . . I sometimes feel they're both as lonely.
Oh well, I guess it's time for bed."
"Phil, if—I mean—tonight I only
Want sleep." "Now what's the matter, Ed?
Don't you—" "I do, Phil, but—" "But what?" "It's
Just that—" "Rowena?" "No, it's not. It's
Too hard to—look, I can't explain."
"Ed, don't play games with me again."
"I love you, Phil—but my desire
Goes beyond sex. Lovers indeed
Must shed more than their clothes. They need
To shed their bodies. Flesh and fire
Can meet but can't merge. It's a state
Only our souls can consummate.

182

8.20   If lovers cannot cease caressing,
        Isn't it that they long to find
        Their bodies' unity expressing
        A truer unison of mind?
        For us this oneness is reality.
        Can't we dispense with the banality
        Of intermediary ends?
        Phil, let's just—why can't we be friends—
        And find this craved complementation
        Of our true selves in its true form,
        The love that keeps our spirits warm
        Through the shared touch of conversation?"
        Phil's eyes have filled with troubled pain.
        He thinks, "Oh no, Ed. Not again."

8.21   Ed says, "You're sad, Phil. I can't bear it
        To see your eyes look so disturbed,
        As if, endeavoring to share it,
        I've let my heart run wild, and curbed
        All your ebullience and elation."
        "Well, Ed, search out your own salvation,"
        Phil answers harshly: "Since your charm
        Will keep you fairly safe from harm,
        And you've insured yourself with heaven,
        Do me the courtesy to abstain
        From commentary on my pain.
        I'm off to bed. It's past eleven.
        Sleep on the bed, or on the floor,
        Whichever boosts your godly score."

8.22   "Phil—" Ed holds Philip's shoulder tightly:
"Sit down. Don't go. Don't talk like that."
"Like what?" retorts Phil, his teeth whitely
Gnawing his lip: "You want more chat,
More Bible bilge to get your rocks off?
Well, I am going to get my socks off.
Don't fool yourself that I'm aggrieved.
Ed, I'm a lot more bored than peeved.
Good night, sweet prince. Say a Hail Mary
For my benighted soul, but please
Keep your bloodcurdling sympathies
Out of my ears. And now, Good Fairy,
Flit as you like with your limp wand—
I'm sleepy, and I can't respond."

8.23   Ed, with a right hook swift and vicious,
Knocks Phil down. Dazed, Phil makes a slow
Lunge for Ed, who, with adventitious
Timing, swerves straight into the blow.
Phil grabs him by the throat, half throttling
Him with the fury he's been bottling.
Now Ed's on top, his jaw contused,
And Phil's left eye and cheek are bruised.
He tries to struggle, but Ed, younger
And stronger, keeps him pinned. But now
Quite suddenly—and God knows how—
As if their unrequited hunger
For blood's assuaged, the murderous peers
Start laughing through their angry tears.

8.24   Ed feels his jaw. Then, dazed and shaking,
Gets up. Phil views the mess around—
Books, Scrabble tiles. . . . His eye is aching.
Ed picks a bookend off the ground.
Phil says, "Don't bother, Ed, just set it
Back on that shelf—no, no, I'll get it. . . .
Now sit down." Phil too sits down; and
Murmuring, "Ed, give me your hand,"
Rests his left cheek against it, closing
His eye that's pulsing black with pain.
"My fault, Ed. I won't yell again.
Now what was it you were proposing
Before our intermission?" "Just
That you don't treat me with disgust."

8.25   Phil slowly says, "If I was saddened—
And caustic, maybe, too—well, yes,
I guess I was, Ed—I was maddened
By hearing your loved voice express
Your own contempt for our lovemaking.
Crass lust—when every time I'm taking
You in my arms, thinking how true,
How clear, how fine our love is, you
Are thinking—what?—that this explosion,
This passing twitch blasphemes God's will—
That we are pigs drunk on our swill
And filth—and that your soul's corrosion
Goes so deep, you must hide and flee
To some dark cave of sanctity?

185

8.26   Why, Ed? These aren't the Middle Ages.
This is the twentieth century.
What facet of our love outrages
Your puritanical purity?
Your church itself is strict or lenient
According to what's most convenient—"
"Phil, that's not so. It's crystal clear
To anyone who is sincere
And doesn't start from scorn, the church's
Teachings are much the same as when
Christ came to save his fellowmen.
It is a rock. You think it lurches
With every fad? Well, read some more
Church history, and you'll learn the score."

8.27   "So, Ed, what is your conscience urging?
That you be chaste your whole life through?
That's mad!" "Jerome, though, died a virgin."
"Too bad that that's too late for you."
Ed frowns: "I can still strive for purity
Of heart—" "...While in its sweet maturity
Your lovely body dries unused?
Ed, if that's so, you'll have abused
Your self—and God's gift—far more truly
Than any flagrant sensualist.
Does earthly beauty just exist
For contemplation? Why, unduly,
Would God create a perfect form
If not to make our lives more warm?

8.28   It seems to me a curious fashion
         To give a man an appetite,
         Then tell him a starvation ration
         Is all he's due for. I don't quite
         Get why religion makes you grateful.
         I would say, Ed, that it's a hateful,
         A pretty odious-spirited trick
         To make you as you are, then stick
         The pin of infinite damnation
         Into you. Tell me what you've done
         That you should need forgiveness. None
         Of those stock yarns of explanation
         About the Fall of Man will do.
         What have you done? And I mean you.

8.29   Is this self-knowledge so reliable?
         Aren't your *ad gloriam*s an excuse?
         Isn't, while you invoke the Bible,
         A chastity belt its actual use?
         And if that fails, there's compensation:
         In Dostoevskian prostration
         You can confess: your soul is sick,
         And you're a worm. A glorious trick!
         It serves to make your conscience calmer,
         Your sins more piquant when you fall,
         And gives you, for no cost at all,
         Your weekly shot of melodrama—
         With a chained audience; while you play
         Lead role, the priest can't run away...."

8.30   Ed sits, white-knuckled, eyes aglitter
With anger as he hears his friend.
Phil's arguments sound strangely bitter.
Determined now to make an end
Of this whole wretched, drawn-out topic,
He seems to shed his philanthropic,
Contained demeanor, and to act
As overwrought as Ed, in fact:
". . . You know, Ed, sometimes you resemble
Some sensitive fanatic ass
Still stuck in catechism class.'
Ed's eyes grow dark, and his lips tremble:
"Is that the best you can distill
About religious feeling, Phil?"

8.31   He speaks to Phil, but cannot face him.
Phil glances at his injured face.
A sudden impulse to embrace him
Arrests his heart, but can't displace
What now amounts to an obsession
To clear the agenda at this session.
He says: "No, Ed. It's that you act
Like some goddamned religious tract.
How long will you keep contemplating
The universe in Gothic font?
Ed, you just don't know what you want.
That's what is so exasperating.
One day we're lovers, and the next
I'm gagged with sacramental text."

8.32   Ed thinks: "And your robust assurance,
Your self-accepting psychic bounce
Frustrates me sometimes past endurance."
He says, "Phil, don't you have an ounce
Of doubt? uncertainty? anxiety?"
"At least it isn't clogged with piety.
Must we go on in this way, Ed?
Let's have a clean affair instead
Of this mud-spattered and moronic
Farce where all passion is denied."
Ed says: "I just can't, Phil. If I'd
Not tried to keep our love platonic,
I'd have debased myself, and been
False to my reason, and unclean.

8.33   As someone skilled in charioteering
By rein and will and effort must
Control his horses' frantic rearing,
The body's turbulence and lust
Must yield to reason's interventions.
Chrysostom, following Plato, mentions—"
"Fuck Chrysostom. Fuck all the fools
Who play the game by others' rules. . . .
You have a mind too, Ed. Why don't you
Go by what *your* heart says is right?
Do you remember our first night?
Do you remember it? Why won't you
Defer to that strong love instead
Of spectral voices in your head?

8.34   Your weekly whims and oscillations
        Will drive me crazy. Help me, Ed—
        I can't subsist on conversations
        When what I need. . . . I've never said
        It's such a big deal, but by hammering
        On this one nail, you've got me clamoring
        For—Ed, it's just absurd to keep
        A sword between us when we sleep.
        When your heart's aching with desire,
        Should something that you've somewhere read
        By someone two millennia dead
        Convince you that your heart's a liar
        And that the truth's this rigmarole
        Of dogma, charioteers, and soul?

8.35   Let me say something that will free you,
        Whichever fork you choose. Love's whole
        Or else it's nothing. I can't see you,
        Ed, as this disembodied soul.
        I cannot fracture my emotions
        Or twist delight to mystic notions.
        What I now feel, I won't hold back.
        What we once shared, I cannot hack
        In bleeding chunks out of my cortex.
        Give me your hand, Ed . . . God, it's cold!"
        "I guess so." Ed withdraws his hold
        And pulls back from the swiftening vortex
        In desperate strokes, till he's on shore,
        Trembling, but steadier than before.

8.36 No more to say. They change. Unsleeping,
      On the same bed they lie apart
      (What terrifying miles), each keeping,
      Unshared, his bitterness of heart,
      The longing each feels for the other,
      Their unburnt love. Perhaps another
      —Who knows—attempt by Phil to touch
      His shivering friend—Is it too much
      To ask of him?—could still unite them;
      But obdurate now, he won't plead,
      Demean his pride, reveal his need . . .
      A hundred reasons—why recite them?
      Ed falls asleep at last, but Phil,
      At two, at three, is wakeful still.

8.37 Wakeful by the loved body, hours,
      Hours to lie, untouched, apart,
      While memory's unpitying powers
      Gouge out the past, and lost thoughts start,
      Shaming the will with their insistence,
      Against all counter of resistance. . . .
      At dawn, Phil falls into a sleep
      That's as exhausted as it's deep.
      When he wakes, Ed has packed. "That glowing
      Black eye—what will you say to Paul?"
      "Don't know. And you?" "A drunken brawl. . . .
      Phil, you'll discover easygoing
      Refreshment soon, I know. It's I . . ."
      "Ed, close the subject." "Right. Good-bye."

Nine

9.1   Impervious to pleas and pity,
        To tender bribes and winning wiles,
        The stratagems of Psycho-Kitty,
        Lamb, catnip, scratching post, and smiles,
        Charlemagne in his guts and sinews
        Detests John still, and John continues
        To rave whenever wronged, and flail
        His arms around his head, assail
        His foe with missiles and invective,
        And mutter, "It's that cat or me,.
        Liz . . . Lizzie, darling, can't you see
        Beyond that mentally defective
        Moth-eaten teddy bear to what
        A swollen cyst of spite he's got?"

9.2   "John, darling, try to understand him.
He's a brave, fine, and useful cat."
"He'd be more useful if I canned him
For rat food—though I doubt a rat
Could stand the stench—Liz, it's pathetic
That this senescent, enuretic,
Ungrateful flea pad is our pet.
He's had a long life. We should get
Rid of—" John stops as Liz stares wildly
At his flushed face. She turns to go,
Then, turning back, exclaims, "You know,
He's always acted pretty mildly
Before you first moved in with me...."
"I see." "You don't see." "Yes I see.

9.3   You cat freaks are, quite simply, crazy.
You'd weep more tears for one lost pet
Than for a flood in Sulawesi.
It serves me right—that's what I get
For thinking I had your affection.
Well, next time, greater circumspection
Is what is called for..." "Stop it, John—
When you go on and on and on
I love you, but I just can't stand you.
I'm going out to buy some steak
And bread, and take a walk...." "Well, take
Your anti-nuclear cat to brand you
With Agent Orange—that's a name
More suited to his joyless frame."

9.4　"Good plan. I think I will." Liz leaves him
　　　To chafe alone against his wrongs.
　　　Suddenly everything aggrieves him:
　　　Cat, house, work, Liz's tuneless songs,
　　　Her tofu-eating, kefir-drinking,
　　　Her "Darling, what have you been thinking?"—
　　　Quirks that delighted him at first,
　　　Through the months' mill wheels suffer worst
　　　Of all the bills of love discounted—
　　　The bills and coos of dateless love.
　　　Alas, alas, as high above . . .
　　　—To quote—"As high as we have mounted . . .
　　　(Ah, Wordsworth!) . . . do we sink as low";
　　　And John finds it indeed is so.

9.5　These pretty whims that used to rivet
　　　His eyes so fondly on Liz now
　　　Convince him that she's off her pivot.
　　　Why else would she so thwart him? How,
　　　Ignoring clear empirical data
　　　Of felony (which that man-hater,
　　　The miscreant cat, leaves everywhere
　　　From soggy duvet to mauled chair),
　　　Can Liz eschew all objectivity,
　　　All logic, every legal trait,
　　　To justify or mitigate
　　　That scumbag's every vile proclivity?
　　　Could he have known, when first they met,
　　　This amnesty she'd grant her pet?

9.6   He mopes around, distraught, distracted;
      Tries to read, can't, looks out: the sky,
      Birdless, unclouded, blue, refracted
      Through the day's smooth lens, strikes his eye.
      He sighs, gets up, puts on a sweater,
      An easier pair of shoes. "I'd better
      Leave this apartment for a bit
      Or I'll—" But as he tries to fit
      The wrong key in the lock, a yellow
      Volkswagen halts and blares its horn
      With the wild will of the newborn.
      "For Christ's sakes! What's wrong with that fellow?
      Hey, stop that—Oh, it's Phil—hey, hi...."
      "Hi, John, I just thought I'd drop by.

9.7   How are you? How's Liz? How's it going?"
      "OK. She's out. And pretty good—
      I guess." "You guess?" "Sure." "Well, you're showing
      Signs of acute strain." "Phil, we should
      Go for a walk—look, don't be lazy—
      Staying in there will drive me crazy."
      "What's happened, John?" "A lovers' tiff.
      It's not worth mentioning...." "Bullshit! If
      You keep on clenching and unclenching
      Your fists like that, it's best to say
      What's on your mind. And anyway
      I'm curious now...." "I've had a drenching
      In the cold spring of Truth." "What's that?"
      "That—more than me—Liz loves that cat."

9.8   "I knew you never loved that cat, John."
"Come on, Phil, you know what I mean."
"Well, I don't see what's wrong with that, John!
You're the intruder on the scene.
It's not unfair . . ." "But how could Lizzie . . ."
"I think it shows that she's not dizzy
In her affections that she won't
Jettison Charlemagne." "Phil, don't
Defend her . . ." "John, I don't care greatly
Whose side I'm taking. With a friend
You ought to speak your mind. I tend
To think a mere Johnny-come-lately,
However much he pleads and plots,
Can't be the one to call the shots."

9.9   John frowns. A premature but mellow
Carved pumpkin grins down from a high
Bow window. Ginkgos, green and yellow,
Trace fall's itinerary. A spry
October breeze gusts up and blusters.
The pyracantha, whose red clusters
Blackbirds get stoned on till they lurch
Unsteadily about in search
Of their lost nests, is now fermenting
Its friable pulp, and bumbling bees
Hum round the pomegranate trees;
And resinous cedars, gently scenting
The sun-seeped air, anesthetize
The garish sumac's autumn dyes.

9.10   John frowns. "I guess I never knew that
        A cat's designs could scupper mine.
        One lives and learns. Of course, it's true that
        Everything still may work out fine—
        And so I sometimes think it's foolish
        To lay down terms. Why be so mulish
        When, given time . . . yet, as Keynes said,
        In the long run we are all dead.
        It's not just that, though, Phil. My freedom
        To be alone—to watch football—
        And to eat junk food . . . these days all
        I do is *buy* books. I can't read 'em.
        I'm dragged off to some dumb ballet,
        Some feeble concert, or worse play.

9.11   It's not that we don't love each other.
        We're a good match: Liz dresses well;
        She's dynamite in bed—but, brother!
        Her cerebellum's shot to hell.
        I never thought I'd have a roomie
        Who whimpered like a goddamned doomie!"
        "A doomie?" "You know—someone who
        Thinks all Jane Fonda says is true.
        She has these exhibitionistic
        Extravagant compulsions—that
        Spiel of the anti-nuclear cat
        Is just one instance: journalistic
        Inanity, but all the same
        She loved that fizzy gulp of fame."

9.12   "And Charlemagne?" "To give him credit,
He mauled the press photographer
Who bumptiously presumed to edit
His pose by fluffing up his fur...."
Phil laughs as John goes on describing
The bitterness he's been imbibing,
And offers sympathy, advice,
Encouragement, and all things nice
That he can give without betraying
His own beliefs; and by and by
John simmers down.... "But, Phil, your eye!"
"Oh, that? That's nothing! You were saying..."
"No, Phil, your left eye looks a bit
Contused." "It's odd you noticed it..."

9.13   "How did it—" "Can you see it clearly?"
"Oh no, it's very faint—but if
You're at this angle..." "So it's nearly..."
"What was it, Phil—a lover's tiff?"
"I ... guess so." "When?" "Last week." "Fantastic!
You've gone back to your orgiastic
Pre-Claire routine! Now, play by play,
And man to man, let's hear..." "No way!
It's private." "Nonsense!" John says, frowning:
"You've grilled me—come on—fair is fair—
Shake off that surreptitious air.
Who did that to you? Quit the clowning!"
"Who do you think?" "I must confess
I can't so much as start to guess...."

9.14   . . . Someone I know?" "Yes." "So I've seen her."
       "Not quite, but—" "Sue?" "No." "Rose?" "No." "*Jan*
       "You're on the wrong track." "Not Rowena?"
       "No." "Phil, I give up." "Ed's the man."
       "Ed?" "Yes." "You *don't* mean Ed." "Yes." "Jesus!"
       "Don't gape at me—I'm not a rhesus
       Monkey with AIDS." "Oh, Jesus, Phil!
       You mean that . . . It's not possible. . . ."
       John stammers, shakes his head; then, shivering,
       Emits a small bleat of disgust
       At this malformed and sickening lust,
       And turns away; while Philip, quivering,
       Feels his fists clench and disengage
       In insult and astonished rage.

9.15   "Oh, Jesus, Phil—but you were married!"
       "Thanks, John, it had escaped my mind."
       "But—I see why the thing miscarried—
       Oh, Jesus, Phil—what do you find
       In—What do two men *do* together?"
       "Try it yourself sometime. But whether
       You do or don't—I doubt you will—
       Stop whimpering, 'Oh, Jesus, Phil!'
       That makes me sick. What you require
       Is a brain transplant. How you dare
       To diagnose my love for Claire
       . . . (And at this point Phil's voice climbs higher
       In fury) . . . I too must confess
       I can't so much as start to guess."

9.16 As brother grimaces at brother
      When a dense veil of hate descends,
      They stare with loathing at each other
      Who just two minutes past were friends.
      Instinctively together turning
      Back to the house, the car, discerning
      With instinct what the other feels,
      They walk in silence. John's head reels:
      "He was my roommate while at college—
      Thank God he didn't. . . . I'd have knocked
      His head off. . . ." Phil, enraged and shocked,
      Thinks, "John's a fool for all his knowledge—
      And, what is worse, a cruel fool
      With the compassion of a mule."

9.17 They're at the door. John, hesitating,
      Straining against himself to see
      Past the revulsion insulating
      Him from all warmth and sympathy
      Toward his friend, feels bound to utter,
      "Well . . . come in." Phil begins to mutter
      A brusque excuse; but with a grin
      Liz, from a window, waves them in:
      "Come in, you guys. I was just baking
      Bran muffins. . . . Good to see you, Phil!
      She thinks: "Do I detect a chill—
      Or is that the attorney making
      Unwarranted deductions? No—
      It really looks as if it's so."

9.18   Inside, John mutters, "Quite delicious."
        Phil growls, "Delicious! Got to go."
        Liz muses, "More and more suspicious."
        Phil rises: "Getting late, you know!"
        Liz frowns: "All right, but your permission
        To leave depends on one condition:
        Tell me what you two talked about.
        You looked so stern when I looked out."
        John blanches: "Nothing!" Liz laughs, taking
        His hand in hers: "Now, that's a lie.
        Well, Phil?" "Oh, just that Ed and I
        Had an affair!" But John, now quaking
        With anger barely in his rein
        Blurts before Liz can speak again:

9.19   "I'm going out—I just can't take this
        . . . (He stands) . . . You've got your answer. Glad?"
        Liz says, "John—John—for goodness' sake, this
        Isn't the way—it's not that bad.
        Look, Phil's your friend—" John shouts, dumbfounded:
        "And Ed's your brother! I'm astounded
        That you can act so cool when he
        And Phil—. . . (He shudders helplessly.) . . .
        Anything goes in this damned city.
        Your brother's either sick or mad
        —And you know what? You're just as bad
        —And your gross cat—It's a real pity
        Ed hasn't seen a shrink—And you
        . . . (He turns on Phil) . . . should see one too!"

9.20   Phil gets up and walks out. Liz, dizzy
       With disbelief, sits still, and stares.
       John looks at her: "Oh, don't sulk, Lizzie.
       I didn't throw him out." Liz glares:
       "Well, don't you think that Phil's offended?"
       "Liz, he offended you. It's splendid
       How you can blame me...." "What's the use?
       Christ, sometimes, John, you're so obtuse!"
       Liz stands up with abrupt decision.
       She's hoping—how, she does not know—
       She can bring peace: that Phil, although
       No doubt concussed from the collision
       Can somehow still be mollified.
       His yellow car's still parked outside.

9.21   Head on the steering wheel, Phil's shaking.
       Liz walks outside and murmurs, "Phil?"
       He looks up, sees her. "If you're making
       Ambassadorial goodwill
       Gestures for John...." Liz says, "I'm really
       Here for myself—and I'm sincerely
       Sorry, Phil—look, unlock this door—
       Thanks ... (Liz gets in) ... I knew the score
       A month ago." Now Phil's incredulous.
       "That Ed..." "That you and Ed..." "You *knew*?
       You mean, Ed spilled the beans to you?"
       "You did, as well. Though fairly sedulous,
       Sunday before the equinox
       You both wore the same mismatched socks."

9.22   Phil looks at Liz with awe: "Amazing!
        We thought that we were so discreet!"
        "Forensic training," Liz states, gazing
        Out of the window at the street,
        Where near the curb a few late flowers,
        Survivors of pre-winter showers,
        Clusters of lilies of the Nile—
        Dark-foliaged, purple—reconcile
        The gazer to the hardening season.
        Liz says, "The last days of the sun.
        We ought to savor them, each one.
        I wish we could—well, there's no reason
        Why we should not—drive to the bay
        And take a walk. What do you say?"

9.23   "Sure, Liz," Phil smiles in admiration.
        He starts the car. "...And, by the way,
        I owe you my appreciation
        For visiting Paul the very day
        That you returned from Lungless." "Really,
        It wasn't much—John and I merely
        Decided we'd drive down to dine
        On the peninsula, and combine...."
        "Well, Paul was very pleased." "Rowena
        Asked after you." "Ah, yes, she tried
        To march with us—but her van died
        Halfway to Lungless. So you've seen her?"
        "That's right," Liz murmurs: "She was there
        At the Lamonts'. What lovely hair!"

9.24   "Er, yes," Phil says: "I sometimes wonder
If I am quite enough for Paul.
He disobeys me—all my thunder
And static has no force at all.
I'm not much good as a role model."
"Why not?" "For one thing, I don't toddle
In time to laws I don't like." "Phil,
Your son will grow up fine. He will.
Who knows—the fact you're demonstrating
May help to save him from the ranks
Of ostrich-humans." "Thanks—and thanks
For the two *Tintin*s. Paul's ingesting
That glorious goop with as much joy
As I did when I was a boy."

9.25   Liz laughs, "So you were brought up on it?
I was, as well. What marvelous books.
I wish someone would write a sonnet
About them. I'm on tenterhooks
Whenever each new one's translated!
I think they're more sophisticated
Than Asterix—and far more fun."
"So do I—Liz, which was the one
In which Bianca Castafiore,
With 'O my beauty past compare'
Lures the Police Chief to her lair?"
Liz laughs, "I don't recall that story. . . .
Wait! Wait! I sense a sudden flash
—By the whiskers of Kürvi-Tasch—

9.26   Wasn't it *King Ottokar's Sceptre?*"
Phil frowns: "Oh, it's too long ago! . . .
I once worked out who was inepter,
Thomson—or Thompson." "Who?" "You know,
I think it was . . . no, I've forgotten.
Thundering typhoons! What a rotten
Memory—Liz—I can't believe
That both of us. . . ." And the two grieve
That that bright world, so just and splendid,
Of Haddock, Gorgonzola, Wagg,
Moon rockets, grog, Red Rackham's swag,
And foul-mouthed parrots could have ended
In adulthood, where truth and light
Do not win out as if by right.

9.27   Phil asks Liz how she came to be there
That day at Lungless. Liz says, "Well,
Those books you left inveigled me there.
John didn't read them. . . . I could tell
You were—surprised." "I was. Belated
Congratulations—your speech rated
An A plus—meaty and concise."
"And how was prison?" "Paradise!
Like-minded souls in dense proximity—
Juggling, hair-braiding, foot massage—
We did our own things, by and large,
And worked plans out with equanimity,
By, as they say, consensus—whence
We formed the new verb: 'to consense.' "

9.28   They park the car by the Marina.
        The surface of the cobalt bay
        Is flecked with white. The moister, keener
        October air has rinsed away
        The whispering mists with crisp intensity
        And over the opaque immensity
        A deliquescent wash of blue
        Reveals the bridge, long lost to view
        In summer's quilt of fog: the towers,
        High-built, red-gold, with their long span
        —The most majestic spun by man—
        Whose threads of steel through mists and showers,
        Wind, spray, and the momentous roar
        Of ocean storms, link shore to shore.

9.29   Gulls veer and scream. As they go strolling
        Along the bay to Fort Point, as
        The noonday sun glints off the rolling
        Wake of a yacht by Alcatraz,
        Liz touches on the electricity
        Sparked off by Charlemagne's publicity—
        Not at home only, but at work:
        When senior partners, whom her "quirk
        Of judgment" startled to the lining
        Of their three-piece suits, told her she
        "Must cease forthwith," Liz quietly
        Informed them she would be resigning
        "As of next month" if they construed
        Her private actions as imbued

9.30   With unprofessional indiscretion,
Especially since (—and here they went
From beet to gray in swift succession—)
She sought their leave to represent
—On an unpaid and independent
Basis, of course—the odd defendant
Who, as she saw it, fell between
Conscience and law. Liz would have been,
She reckons, fired in a second
Had tokendom—she was the sole
Woman attorney in the whole
Ivied establishment—not beckoned.
Starched stiff with reprehension, they
Frowned, fumed, and let her have her way.

9.31   "So if you think it's advantageous,"
Liz says, "feel free to pick my brains."
Phil laughs: "You really are courageous!"
Liz blushes, and then ascertains
The details of the mass arraignment.
"What's your aim, Phil," she asks, "attainment
Of a good verdict—or good press?"
Phil says, "Well, really both, I guess.
But surely there's no contradiction?"
"Well, not as such," Liz says, and smiles,
"But some flamboyant courtroom wiles
Enhance your chances of conviction.
Play to the gallery, and the judge
May treat the whole defense as fudge."

9.32　　They wander for a while, not saying
　　　　Too much, then stroll out on the pier
　　　　By Old Fort Point. Surfers, displaying
　　　　Sinuous equestrianism, steer
　　　　Their boards on the in-pouring rollers;
　　　　On shore, the eight-year-old controllers
　　　　Of motley skateboards swiftly skim
　　　　In competition bright and trim
　　　　Past fishermen, gulls, rocks, and breakers,
　　　　While high above the Golden Gate,
　　　　Nestling the fort, in unornate
　　　　Magnificence across the acres
　　　　Of whitecapped sea, the golden span
　　　　Hangs for the world to hymn and scan.

9.33　　They climb the cliff to its approaches
　　　　And start to walk across the bridge
　　　　To the Marin shore, when Liz broaches,
　　　　Without the fluff of verbiage,
　　　　The subject that, once manifested
　　　　A month ago, has since arrested,
　　　　On one trained spot, her stethoscope
　　　　Of sisterly concern: "I hope
　　　　You two are suited for each other."
　　　　Phil hesitates, then starts to speak,
　　　　"I doubt it, Liz. I felt last week
　　　　I'd never understand your brother.
　　　　He's heaven-struck. What are the odds
　　　　Of mortals versus saints and gods?"

208

9.34   Liz laughs, "Consorting with celestial
        Beings is typical of Ed."
        Phil grimaces, "Where we weak bestial
        Affective devils fear to tread—
        In terror lest some gross tumescence
        Should jar the luculent quintessence
        Of little Rupert Brooke. Oh, Liz—
        I love the bastard, but he is
        So inaccessible: pollution
        Is all he—maybe that's why he's
        Keen on a nuclear power freeze—
        I doubt that any elocution
        Of mine could . . ." "Phil, give Ed a chance.
        He's young; I'm sure he'll change his stance.

9.35   You know, he sees you as heroic. . . ."
        Phil sighs, "That's finished. As for me,
        Try wrestling with Paleozoic
        Concepts of sin from ten to three
        On Friday night—Christ, I'm so lonely—
        This past year's been—God knows I only
        Want to—O God knows what—to live
        Without this emptiness—to give
        A little love, to get a little.
        He's got his thoughts, though; I've got mine.
        We're through, Liz; I don't mean to whine
        About how unjust life is—it'll
        Hurt less with time, I know, somehow.
        But we both know it's over now."

9.36   Liz sighs, and Phil resumes, "I shouldn't
Be talking this way, least of all
With you, Liz—I'm upset—I wouldn't
Have brought it up if. . . ." With a small,
A gentle nod of comprehension
Liz looks away while with some tension
Her own hand grips the low guardrails.
"I think that . . ."—and her voice now fails—
". . . I think I understand the feeling."
Then, with an effort: "Well, love's fun
At first . . . but living with someone
You love can be less than appealing
If everything's just great in bed
Yet nothing's shared inside your head."

9.37   Phil says, "You know, Liz, this rigidity
Of John's is less a function of
Innate intemperate rabidity
Than of a childhood lack of love. . . ."
(He meditates that what's ironic
Is that their sudden and cyclonic
Soap opera should whirl and blare
Above a now-defunct affair.
Odd too that John, with all his learning,
Who likes Brahms, reads Mann, and quotes Keynes,
And who not long since honed his brains
At Berkeley of all places, burning
With moral odium thus should rend
His friendship with his oldest friend.)

9.38   Liz adds, "You're right, Phil. John's not vicious—
Or unaffectionate or unkind.
He's generous, he's not malicious.
It's that at times he's almost blind.
I've got my share of immaturity
And silliness and insecurity—
But John finds every quirk a goad
To make him bubble or explode.
Though he's himself as self-divided
As me—or anyone—he fails
To comprehend this when he flails
His cutlass round; if less one-sided,
I'd take his jokes in better part...."
She reins her thoughts back with a start....

9.39   "But, Phil—we shouldn't be dissecting
Those whom we love behind their backs."
"Oh, I don't know," says Phil, reflecting,
"I now yearn less for heart attacks,
Passion's angina, and love's blindness
Than company and warmth and kindness.
Perhaps I'm harder to disarm,
And cherish courage more than charm...."
He looks at Liz. "... I'm only speaking
For myself, Liz." Liz turns away
And gazes out across the bay
To where a band of smog lies, streaking
The Oakland hills with a low haze,
And as she speaks her voice betrays

9.40 Her pain—that she's almost betraying
      Lover, and brother: "Phil, don't say
      Words that, once said, there's no unsaying.
      We should walk back. Who knows—things may
      Get better. . . . Anyway, it's Sunday.
      Let's cross the bridge: this is the one day
      Of the whole week the seaward view
      Is open." Phil smiles. "Saturday too."
      They cross. The westward arc of ocean
      Beyond Point Lobos gleams with light.
      Phil lifts a hand to shield his sight,
      And Liz with quietened emotion
      Asks him how Paul is, and they talk
      With their old ease, along their walk.

Ten

10.1 The clapboard church with the white steeple
   On a gray, frozen day extrudes
   A complement of cheerful people;
   Resuscitating platitudes
   With neighborly conviviality,
   They thank God that his liberality
   Has touched their valley's ripening vines.
   If for Thanksgiving he assigns
   A sunless mist, that is small reason
   To cavil at his subtle ways—
   For this last month's unbroken rays
   Of sunshine sweetened the slow season
   To a grand harvest, nonpareil
   For cabernet and zinfandel.

10.2 All the Doratis and their neighbors
   (Whose scattered clans rejoin today)
   Rest from their individual labors
   And go to church to nod or pray.
   They mill outside now that Thanksgiving
   Service is over, now the living
   Vines are asleep, and the repair
   Of harvesting machines, the care
   Of injured tractors, and the tending
   Of the new crush (for those whose crop
   Ferments in fragrance, drop on drop
   In their own cellars) mark the ending
   (A day of pious, ritual cheer
   And gossip) of the vineyard year.

10.3 Old Mike Dorati, who's been farming
   His benchland loam for forty years,
   Doffs his hat briskly as the charming
   Bevy of Levasseurs appears:
   Juliet, Judy, and Joanna,
   Each head draped in a silk bandanna,
   Escorted by their parents, breeze
   Out of the church; and by degrees
   The sky thins and the sunlight glistens
   On the white steeple and the vines,
   The misted redwoods and moist pines,
   While Mike Dorati coughs and listens
   To Peter Levasseur complain
   Of winter's harsh forecast of rain.

214

10.4   "It's nothing short of devastating.
        Last year we lost our best topsoil...."
        While Levasseur's cheeks glow, berating
        The storms that threaten to despoil,
        With coursing floods, the hillside reaches
        Of his merlot, Mike says, "That teaches
        You, Pete, to plan a bit ahead.
        You should have planted—as I've said
        To you ten thousand times—that fescue
        Along your rows, and near that pipe—
        I'll show you how—and look, don't gripe
        At the deaf sky when you can rescue
        Your miracle mud through your own toil.
        Just grow that grass and hold that soil....

10.5   ... Liz, Ed, Sue, I'm just going over
        To Pete's.... Where's Mom? Art? John? ... OK!
        I'll try to be home soon.... No, clover
        Won't mat it in that stable way.
        If I were you...." They leave their father
        And drive back home. Sue says, "I'd rather
        Dad quit consulting for a day.
        How often do we come to stay?"
        Ed shrugs: "Guess he's a workaholic."
        "But on Thanksgiving? People take
        Advantage of him." "Hey, don't make
        A martyr out of Dad. To frolic
        Knee-deep in mud in place of rest
        Is just the sport that he likes best....

10.6   ... But, Sue, please help me solve a mystery."
"Sure, Ed." "Well, Sue, it deals with Art,
Your ardent fan of local history
And the mild mango of your heart."
"What about him?" "Well," Ed says, sighing,
"How can one man be—without trying—
So boring, doughy, stiff, and weak?"
Liz frowns, and gives Ed's nose a tweak:
"You little beast—he isn't boring."
Sue punches him. Ed holds her arm:
"Ouch, sis, I didn't mean no harm!
Sure, I don't like his violent snoring
And his fat smirk—but that apart,
I really don't object to Art."

10.7   Back at the ranch, with two prospective
Sons-in-law wandering in train,
Mrs. Dorati, with reflective
Pauses to ease arthritic pain,
Walks slowly to the graystone winery,
Flame-red in its autumnal finery
Of Boston ivy, through the fields
Of straggling splendor whose air yields
The late rich musk of grapes decaying
Into the earth, leaves trampled down
To humus, and the tattering brown
Vine bark, its darkened scars betraying
The vines' sharp battles, won and lost,
Each year, with virus, pest, and frost.

10.8   Impressed into the preparation
        Of the great feast, the two houseguests
        Drift down a vapid conversation
        Whose stream John suddenly arrests
        By asking Art with a mock-hearty
        Insouciance, "Did Madame Dorati
        By any chance, Art, question you
        About your plans regarding Sue?"
        Art's knife halts its potato-peeling.
        He looks at John and grins: "I'll say!
        So she's begun on you today?"
        And in a flush of fellow feeling
        The two compare notes, and decide
        How many kids each must provide.

10.9   But for duplicative insurance
        Mrs. Dorati's drawn aside
        Her son, whose filial endurance,
        Fancy, and tact are sorely tried
        As he attempts to duck and parry
        Her fervid pleas that he should marry:
        "You shouldn't let time pass you by.
        What girl's the apple of your eye
        Currently, Ed?" "Mom, I'm too busy,"
        Ed groans, "for girls—and all that stuff.
        I'm twenty-three. There's time enough.
        Why don't you hassle Sue or Lizzie?
        Gee—it's already half past one.
        I'll go see if that turkey's done."

10.10   Two hours later, spent and bloated,
Like pythons who have swallowed pigs,
All in the household are devoted
To groaning gently, after swigs,
"What's on TV?" and reminiscing
About old times, friends who are missing,
And movies shot when Ed was two
Of Liz admiring baby Sue.
At last they settle down to viewing
That blood sport, football—in its way
Almost as vicious as croquet—
While Charlemagne's contented mewing
(Tail across paws, and head atilt)
Blends with the coffee's bubbling lilt.

10.11   At each Thanksgiving now he perches
Upon a lower chair, to purr
Out long delight, then yawns, and searches
For his young Persian friend, whose fur
Is black and whose one eye is golden,
And to whom Charlemagne's beholden
For tours of his own old domain:
The Winery Cat, the scourge and bane
Of the upcoming generations
Of upstart field mice who cavort
In the new grass, fresh, green, and short,
That clothes the valley's undulations
In daubs of life among the lines
Of leafless and exhausted vines.

10.12   As for cold Schwarz, the cats ignore him—
        In much the same way that John shrinks
        Whenever Ed attempts to draw him
        Into small talk; they sip their drinks
        And warily appraise each other.
        Meanwhile, Sue's talking to her mother
        About the scholarship she's won
        To go to Paris. "We've begun
        To think we should defer our wedding...."
        Mrs. Dorati's face falls: "Sue!
        On dear! Oh darling, not you too!"
        And starts to cry. She fears she's heading
        Toward a grandchildless last age
        Which no young spirit will assuage.

10.13   She thinks of aches that now beset her,
        That swell her joints with rheumatoid
        Arthritis, the stiff limbs that fetter
        The brisk gait that she once enjoyed—
        The freeing bliss when she would sally
        Out just at dawn into the valley
        Where now at dawn she can't unrein
        Her spirit from her crippling pain.
        Sue strokes her mother's arm and mumbles,
        "Just for a year, Mom, or two years..."
        While by the fire as evening nears,
        Mr. Dorati's bishop stumbles
        Into oblivion, and Liz smiles,
        And spreads curt havoc in his files.

219

10.14   John watches TV; reads; is restive;
            Smiles weakly at old family lore
            With jollity more forced than festive.
            Erratic fragments of speech draw
            His thoughts from their withdrawing orbit:
            "Lemon and salt . . . that should absorb it
            —Or most of it, Mom . . . black ones . . . no,
            You don't need lye . . . Phil told me so. . . .
            I guess you're right—you haven't met him. . . ."
            John's mouth turns southwards in distaste,
            As though a bug that he's erased,
            Half reemerging, will not let him
            Run his clean subroutines at will.
            He thinks: "Get out of my life, Phil."

10.15   John's volatile exasperation,
            His semi-rational unease
            Finds self-fulfilling confirmation
            Wherever his mind turns. He sees
            His friend's impenitent freewheeling
            As weird; when he heard Liz revealing
            That Phil and Ed's affair had died,
            Oddly enough it verified
            The image of a loose careering
            Cannon aboard a listing deck.
            Phil's salvos at High Nuclear Tech—
            And Liz's legal volunteering—
            Oppress John dimly, mind and heart. . . .
            "Coffee?" He comes to with a start.

10.16 Coffee; and eggnog; and as twilight
    Drifts through the trees, and a gold cloud
    Floats singly over the hills to highlight
    The ambient darkness, and a shroud
    Of silence falls upon the nesting
    Birds, and the fevered earth is resting,
    Sue brings her cello down and plays
    A Bach suite that in earlier days
    Her mother loved—and still loves—only
    Where she once smiled, it now ensnares
    Her in a weft of grief. She stares
    Down at her mottled skin, her lonely,
    Bent hands. She thinks: "Don't weep. Don't pray.
    It's pain. It can't be wished away."

10.17 She stares, and memory estranges
    Her from the room, the firelight.
    Like seashells high on snowy ranges,
    Forgotten thoughts return tonight,
    And as her daughter plays, she's drifting
    Back to her childhood, where the shifting
    Silhouettes flung against the wall
    Were those of . . . "Well, but why recall
    . . . (She gently pulls herself together) . . .
    Those times when, with the kids all here
    —God knows where they will be next year
    With Sue in France—and God knows whether
    We'll all be living—I should praise,
    Not fault, these migratory days."

10.18   Now it is midnight, and in keeping
With long-standing Dorati laws,
Each of the visitors is sleeping
In his own upstairs room. Art's snores,
Conducted through the wall, are merging
With John's dreams: now a storm is surging;
Now a slow sea beast snarls and grunts;
And now a railway engine shunts.
John sleeps through all this; and on waking
Heads down for breakfast, where his host
Regales him, over tea and toast,
With brief accounts of tartan-making,
The dusky-footed wood rat, and
The history of the ampersand.

10.19   But all with such a warmth of spirit
That John, though stunned, is charmed. Each wad
Of data shoots past, and to hear it
So beguiles John, he starts to nod,
And yawns a bit and, half addressing
Himself to coffee, tries expressing
His own scant views on this and that.
Mr. Dorati, smiling at
His young friend's spirited demeanor,
Says, "John, I'm pruning vines today.
Why don't you join me. By the way,
Where is my wife? You haven't seen her? . . .
Marie . . . Marie. . . . She likes to walk,
Though lately . . . well, I shouldn't talk

10.20   About such tedious things . . . but lately . . .
       Marie . . . ah, there you are . . . my dear,
       A walk perhaps?" And with the stately
       Decorum of a cavalier
       Gives her his arm. The trio wanders
       Into the vineyard, and Mike ponders
       What to prune first. "I may as well
       Start on this block of zinfandel. . . .
       Shears . . . thanks . . . you know, John, we're attacking
       The core of winemaking today.
       Good pruning—good grapes. And I say:
       Let the grapes speak! Apart from racking,
       Don't fiddle, filter, fuss, or fine—
       You'll leach the zest out of the wine. . . ."

10.21   Mrs. Dorati stands and watches
       As John learns how to clip and prune.
       A willing laborer, though he botches
       A ragged limb or two, he soon
       Snips rough canes through with clean facility,
       Counts spurs for optimal fertility,
       Sweats in the sun and laughs out loud,
       Is callused, weary, pleased, and proud.
       Back in the winery, corks are popping—
       For now, with post-Thanksgiving haste,
       Folk come from near and far to taste
       Dorati reds; and fruit flies, dropping
       In dense and tipsy clusters, seethe
       Round vintages uncorked "to breathe."

10.22   At dusk, the daily round completed,
The company splits into twos:
The cats range in pursuit of fetid
Quarry while Ed and reptile snooze
Before the TV; in the attic
Sue and her boyfriend with ecstatic
Pangs of discovery and rebirth
Sift through an old trunk and unearth
Love letters of Hungarian cousins,
A blind and legless teddy bear
(With a stitched smile that mocks despair),
Two statues of the Buddha, dozens
Of unused stamps from Liechtenstein,
And bills for sacramental wine.

10.23   Down plaited streams of family history,
Alive with flotsam, on they glide!
They try to worry out the mystery
Of the old wine bills and decide
The vineyard's product-mix decision
Veered churchwards during Prohibition.
That solved, Art wonders: "Sue, are these
Two bronzes Japanese or Chinese?"
"Don't know! Too bad Jan couldn't make it
To the vineyard. I did invite ...
But you know Jan ... she said she *might*. ...
As for this teddy bear, let's take it
Down, and ask Dad and Mom if they
Know how it came to be this way."

10.24   Downstairs, Sue's father makes the fire.
"Real gems, our kids!" he says, and looks
At sleeping Ed. The flames rise higher;
The old folks settle down with books:
He with *Tom Jones*, she with a thriller
Entitled *Jack the Lady-Killer*.
Though he reads his, and she reads hers,
From time to time a thought occurs
That must be shared—for instance, whether
Arsenic grows into one's hair—
Or how Tom plots his debonair
And raffish gambits. Thus together
They pool their prose, and intertwine
Their lives along a common vine.

10.25   Outside, the red sky dyes the river
That murmurs down the valley, where
The leafless weeping willows quiver
And where at dusk a shivering hare
May be seen poised or crouched or bounding.
There Liz one spring saw an astounding
And lovely sight just after dawn—
A gray doe suckling her young fawn.
The doe looked round, unagitated
By Liz (then nine), who held her breath,
And who, though frozen half to death,
Volitionlessly stared and waited
Until the fawn had drunk its fill
And doe and fawn slipped off uphill.

10.26   Now she and John are slowly walking
By the red water, hand in hand.
Warmed by the memory, not talking,
Liz slips into that early land;
While John, whose hard-worked limbs are aching,
Senses a broad contentment taking
Him forwards to the future. "Liz,
It strikes me that perhaps it is
Time we two should, well, be more serious.
It's been a year since we first met. . . .
Your folks suggest we ought to get . . ."
He trails off with an unmysterious
Ellipsis, and waits, confident
Of Liz's tremulous assent.

10.27   "Give me some time, John." "Time? But surely—
We love each other well enough. . . .
Why are you acting so demurely?"
Liz says, "There's more to life than love.
I've got to think this out." Still holding
Each other's hand, but with John scolding
Her gently, a bit puzzled, they
Walk homewards by a shorter way
Across the vineyard. As engaging
As at the best of times he is,
He turns to other things; but Liz
Discovers consternation raging
Within her heart, and has no clue
Of what to say, feel, think, or do.

10.28　Next day, by one of life's mischances,
　　　　Mrs. Dorati tries to broach
　　　　The grandchild question. As she glances
　　　　At Liz with unexpressed reproach,
　　　　Liz looks about: cats and iguana
　　　　Lie sunk in somnolent Nirvana
　　　　In sunlight; Ed and Sue have gone
　　　　To fetch the mail; and Art and John
　　　　Can be seen in the distance, pacing
　　　　About the vineyard; and it's clear,
　　　　With no hope of diversion near,
　　　　That Liz is imminently facing
　　　　—Her dad lies dozing in his chair—
　　　　An ordeal that she cannot bear.

10.29　It warms up with the observation
　　　　Of how considerate, how polite,
　　　　How well-dressed, and in conversation
　　　　How well-versed John is, and how bright.
　　　　Liz shuts her book. Her mother, gazing
　　　　Mistily at her spouse, who's lazing,
　　　　Half absent, in his chair, first veers
　　　　To married love, the ripening years,
　　　　The boon of children, how she's yearning
　　　　To see the same joys settle on
　　　　Their lives as well. . . , then brings up John
　　　　Once more—and Liz, her earlobes burning,
　　　　Suddenly rises, and without
　　　　Comment or protest, walks straight out.

10.30   The coda of this brief, upsetting
Duet (for one voice) is observed
By Mike Dorati, who (forgetting
That peace is often better served
Not by alertness but by sleeping
Through all alarms) looks at his weeping
Wife, and his daughter, who now stands,
Her book gripped tightly in her hands,
Immobile, in the dewy cover
Of new grass quilting the long soil
Between the vines; while, in a coil,
A red-winged hawk lists high above her.
He sighs: "I'll talk to Liz, my dear.
Don't be upset, love. You stay here."

10.31   He walks into the vineyard. "Lizzie . . ."
He pats her hand. Her eyes are wet.
"Come, Liz, don't get into a tizzy
For nothing. I know you're upset
About this, but you know your mother. . . ."
He kisses her. ". . . Now, if your brother
And sister shrugged it off, I'm sure
You can as well, my dear. Now you're
The eldest and most understanding. . . .
Mom misses you a lot. This year
You've hardly visited us here.
Not that, my dear, I'm reprimanding,
But you don't realize it can get
Lonely at times. Now I'd just let

10.32   The storm blow over. Liz, remember,
Your mother's aches and pains increase
In winter, and it's late November.
Now go in, darling, and make peace.
And keep off things that could upset her.
She's not got long—I mean, it's better
If you go in and hold her hand . . ."
Liz cuts in: "I don't understand.
She's not got—what?" In sudden terror
She sees her father's face fall. "Dad—"
Though silent, his unfeigning, sad
Eyes hold no hope, no hope of error.
Dry-eyed with pain, at last Liz speaks:
"When did—" "We've known now for some weeks."

10.33   Elsewhere, John's thinking, "What a sunny
Morning this is! I feel today
The world's at peace. I've got a funny
Feeling the tides have turned my way.
It's just as well," he muses breezily,
"That Lizzie didn't yield so easily.
Anticipation's rather nice.
This waiting adds a certain spice. . . .
Inaction's made me quite insightful! . . .
Let me . . . (and here he yawns) . . . salute
Life, liberty, and the pursuit
Of laziness. It's quite delightful!"
He stares at the cerulean sky
And the jet contrails arcing by.

229

10.34 On whether this delirious laziness
       Would please him if extended, John
       Confesses to a certain haziness;
       But right now, as the sunlight on
       The white dew, striking at an angle,
       Unblends on every drop to spangle
       The vineyard with prismatic light—
       Or as a black-swarmed, southward flight
       Of starlings whirs and swirls and clusters
       Like coffee grounds in liquid air,
       All John can do is stand and stare.
       At length, reluctantly, he musters
       The will to go and fetch a file:
       "One hour's work shouldn't cramp my style."

10.35 The mail lies on the front hall table.
       John's curious; he riffles through
       The pile, and murmurs, "Here's a cable;
       For whom? Marie . . . and here are two
       Copies—why two?—of the *Smithsonian*."
       He idly flips through "Amazonian
       Artifacts," "The Cults of Thrace,"
       "Lear's Birds." . . . Out of its hiding place
       Behind the door, with swift propulsion,
       A gray and orange mass streaks by,
       Chased by a black puff with one eye.
       John views the vision with revulsion.
       "Quite a thick letter here for Liz. . . .
       I wonder who its author is."

10.36   The fuzzy postmark's no assistance.
        There's no return address. John thinks,
        "That's odd." And then a frigid distance,
        A disbelieving hatred sinks
        Into his gaze as the handwriting
        Nudges his memory, igniting
        Cold glints of fury in his brain.
        He stands there, scoured with shock and pain.
        Liz enters; as she brushes past him
        To go into the living room
        He grabs her shoulder: "I presume
        You plan to lead him on and cast him
        Off with the same alacrity
        That he's dropped Claire—or you've dropped me.

10.37   Well, I hope you enjoy each other."
        Liz quietly says, "John, let me go. . . .
        I must go in and see my mother."
        John drops his arm. He cries out: "So—
        You don't deny this thing?" Liz, staring
        At John, a desperate, despairing
        Incomprehension in her glance,
        Now slowly winds out of her trance.
        "What is it?" "What? O God! This letter."
        "Who's it from?" "Phil." "What does it say?"
        With jealous loathing and dismay
        John thrusts it in her hands: "You'd better
        Find out yourself. It's your mail." Liz
        Says, "John, I don't know what it is. . . .

10.38   ... Some anti-nuclear stuff? That trial ..."
"Then open it." "Why?" "Open it."
"Not now." "So much for your denial."
"Denial?" "Don't give me that shit!"
Liz cries, "I love you—don't abuse me—
John, I can't take it—don't accuse me
Of having an affair with Phil—
Don't drive me to it—or I will."
And blinded by a fit of weeping,
As if her heart were breaking, she
Makes for the door unsteadily—
And when (a sick repentance seeping
Into John's heart) he tries to clutch
Her hand, she shudders at his touch.

10.39   Mrs. Dorati, driven thither
By John's voice in fortissimo,
Turns from the doorway in a dither
Of indecision. "Mom, don't go—"
Liz sobs, and holds her mother tightly.
Mrs. Dorati gently, lightly,
Passes her hand through Liz's hair,
And Liz, in misery and despair,
Says, "Mom—Dad told me. I'm so sorry
I ran away. I love you so.
You should have told me." "Yes, I know;
I didn't want to cause you worry—
I really don't believe it still. ...
Sometimes I even hope it will

10.40   Just disappear, as if by magic. . . .
          But, Lizzie, I could live for years,
          So, darling, it's not quite as tragic
          As it originally appears.
          It's in the liver. It's not painful.
          It's *these* that. . . ," and with a disdainful
          Look at her knobbled hands, she smiles.
          Up in his room, John packs his files
          And clothes, and thinks: "Thank God I vanished
          When she came in—I hate a scene."
          Soon, grimacing, as if quinine
          Had smeared his teeth, self-damned, self-banished,
          He starts his car. When Ed cries, "Wait!"
          John glares through him with transferred hate.

Eleven

11.1   The clapboard church with the white steeple
       On a gray, frozen day extrudes
       A complement of cheerful people.
       Clicked in expansive attitudes,
       They brave the shriveling church-step weather,
       And later, in bright knots together,
       Crowd the front porch of the vineyard,
       Half bombed, half waiting to bombard
       With hugs, confetti, and confection
       The bride and groom—who've left the church
       And vanished, some suggest, in search
       Of a spot where, without inspection
       By the lewd crowd, a private kiss
       May sanctify their nuptial bliss.

11.2 The paragon of geniality,
   Mr. Dorati now extends
   Epithalamic hospitality
   To neighbors, relatives, and friends:
   "So glad you could . . . oh, thank you, Peter!
   Of course you'll have a chance to greet her. . . .
   Quite sudden, yes . . . but there you are . . .
   Young folks, you know. . . . You're right, it's far
   Too chilly . . . let's go in . . ."; and Mr.
   Dorati guides the Levasseurs
   Toward the cake, while Judy purrs
   To Juliet, her elder sister:
   "I never thought I'd see the sight
   Of Liz Dorati dressed in white."

11.3 Mrs. Dorati's eyes are puffy.
   Rowena's choking back a sob.
   The Winery Cat, with fierce and fluffy
   Abandon, savors glob on glob
   Of cream and chardonnay compounded.
   Now Charlemagne has deftly bounded
   Toward the tall-tiered wedding cake,
   Baroque with maculate swirl and flake
   Of chocolate, marzipan, and icing.
   Though fuddled by the wine he's sipped,
   He notes how Paul and Chuck, equipped
   With knives, are violently slicing
   The cake for human guests to eat;
   And, growling, beats a foiled retreat.

11.4   Old Mrs. Weiss, flown in from Florida,
        Looks furious at the whole affair.
        She meditates: "What could be horrider
        Than Phil divorcing that nice Claire?
        Where's the boy now—and where's this hussy?"
        And hobbling forward, with a fussy
        Impatience brooking no dissent,
        She moves to where her diffident
        Daughter-in-law stands, and with quavering
        Passion exclaims: "Young woman, you
        Have no conception what to do.
        You're not a patch on Claire!" Then, wavering
        —A waiter pouring champagne nears—
        Turns on her heel and disappears.

11.5   Phil, half engaged in self-decrial
        Induced by the champagne he's spilt
        On Joan Lamont, describes his trial:
        "Enough to make an orchid wilt!
        The judge was like a prosecutor.
        He aimed his legalist peashooter
        At every clause of our defense.
        This failed to hold! That made no sense!
        As for the doctrine of necessity,
        It was irrelevant to the case!
        And so this derelict frog-face,
        This ball of ignorant obesity,
        Threatened to send us back to jail. . . ."
        Phil gestures as he tells the tale

11.6   And spills champagne in a new shower
          Upon his friends. "Oh, sorry, Matt. . . .
          The way some folks abuse their power
          Is something to be marveled at! . . .
          Here, have some cake . . . ah, there's my mother. . . ."
          Phil tipsily attempts to smother
          Her with a hug, while with a glare
          She shakes him off, and snorts: "Take care!
          If Paul complains to me about her,
          I'll catch the next flight out . . . you'll see!
          You're a real fool, Phil. As for me
          —And Paul—well, we can do without her. . . ."
          Matt muses, "The señora's drunk.
          She looks as sozzled as a skunk!"

11.7   Ed kisses Liz; with gallant lightness
          He wishes her all happiness.
          He goes to greet Phil, but a tightness
          Within his chest acts to compress
          His breath, and to subvert all action:
          The crowded room—the old attraction—
          Phil drunk—inspirited—merge to move
          Ed's heart toward his former love.
          He stands there wordless, cold, and trembling.
          "What should I do?" he thinks. "Will he
          Embrace me? Shake hands? Speak? All three?"
          Phil turns and sees him; and, dissembling,
          Ed makes a feeble joke about
          Phil's wearing black; and wanders out.

11.8   Free of the smoke, his eyes still smarting,
He breathes the winter vineyard air.
Meanwhile, inside, the toasts are starting.
Now someone laughs—and from somewhere
The clink of glasses, next the quiet
Moments of drinking, then a riot
Of simultaneous speech, the loud
Sound cycles pulse out from the crowd.
Here Mrs. Craven shakes her stogie;
And there, supported by twin sticks,
Old Mr. Cobb, now eighty-six,
Stands, talking to an older fogy
About the happier days of yore:
Of slump, depression, and the war.

11.9   Ed thinks, "I'm acting like a martyr.
Bad form on Liz's wedding day!"
He walks back in. The menacing garter,
The flinging of the white bouquet,
The canapés, the reminiscing,
The crush, the chaos, and the kissing,
The twirling pairs, the tilting cake,
The thirties tunes "for old times' sake,"
The vast permuted introductions
With older couples who appear
To be at ease with no one here,
The contradictory instructions
Fed to the caterers and the band,
Lure Ed back to a brighter land.

11.10   Bewildered by the fraught frivolity
He sees around him, Kim Tarvesh,
A joyless guest amid the jollity,
Dreams of his thesis—that dense mesh,
That spongy marsh of curly deltas
In which all year he wastes and welters.
While round him voices rise and fall
In oral goulash, Occam's call
Leaches his vision of variety:
He mumbles, "In all likelihood
An n-dimensional matrix could
Succinctly summarize society...."
(Poor Kim Tarvesh—we must recall
He's an economist after all.)

11.11   Art laughs, "Well, Jan's not here—you blew it!
So, Sue, you owe me twenty bucks."
Sue looks depressed. "I guess I knew it...
But hoped, perhaps...," and as Art tucks
The bill away says, somewhat sadly,
"I think this thing's been handled badly....
Well, each according to her taste,
But why such unconsidered haste?
It's not like Liz at all...," and, frowning,
Sue bites a leaf of marzipan
And looks at her extended clan:
"Liz seems so happy, though. She's clowning
With Phil now.... Would she carry on
So unconstrainedly with John?"

11.12 Mr. Dorati seeks his daughter
       Amid the crowd and tugs her sleeve:
       "Liz, dear, a word ... (and now he's brought her
       Toward the door) ... Liz, I believe
       That you're aware of what you're doing.
       I'd hate to see you sad, or ruing
       The day that you became a wife....
       You do love Phil?" "Not on your life!"
       Liz giggles: "Oh, Dad, don't look gloomy—
       I like him, though. Here, have some more!"
       And rapidly begins to pour
       The Korbel. "Dad, he's gentle to me."
       "Well, Liz," her father says, perplexed,
       "Should I be pleased, appalled, or vexed?"

11.13 Liz walks toward Phil. She's thinking, "Whether
       It's love or not means nothing much.
       Love by itself's a tightening tether,
       A habit-forming drug, a crutch....
       I like Phil, and he likes and needs me.
       And then, there's Paul too ... and that leads me
       To wonder about Charlemagne.
       ... (She takes Phil's arm, and sips champagne.) ...
       It's a full household. Though I wouldn't
       Say I'm impulsive, and though Dad
       Must think I've lost my head, I'm glad
       We've married with such haste. I couldn't
       Hope for a better better half:
       A good kind man who makes me laugh."

11.14   To link this chapter of the novel
          To John's departure, sketched before,
          Requires a flashback. (I should grovel
          At this cheap stratagem, and, more,
          My bard card should be burned.) Dear Reader,
          In mitigation, let me plead a
          Drainage of brain. Perhaps you'll wait
          Till it's recharged? . . . You indicate
          I must continue with the story?
          ". . . Nae man can tether time or tide;
          The hour approaches Tam maun ride. . . ."
          Well, dinna fidge—I willna bore ye.
          (A safe bet: if you've read till here,
          You must possess an iron ear.)

11.15   Her mother's illness, the traumatic
          Parley with John, Phil's long brief read,
          Left Liz so drained, pale, and erratic
          In thought, mood, look, and word that Ed
          (Himself perplexed by John's behavior)
          Stepped in as psychiatric savior,
          Steeped her with brandy for her good,
          And soothed her, as a brother should.
          Slowly the bruising shock diminished.
          Ed asked her: 'Do you love John still?"
          And Liz in turn asked: "What of Phil?"
          The phrase, "God knows—but that's all finished!"
          Now economically supplied
          The sad response on either side.

11.16   That Monday morning, at the trial
           Of Phil (and four more peaceniks), Liz
           Despite the judge's blunt denial
           Of her chief argument—with fizz
           And flair and vehemence and fury—
           Contrived to split the Lungless jury:
           "You are the judges in this court,
           And no one else!" And so, in short,
           Though somewhat low on legal logic
           (Since the judge ruled she could not plead
           Necessity), Liz veered with speed
           To an assault more demagogic
           And, startlingly, achieved a breach.
           This is a fragment of her speech:

11.17   "... People of Lungless Town! I beg you,
           Don't smile at the malignant growth
           That kills you. Lungless Labs may egg you
           —With business, Uncle Sam, or both—
           To take their word God's imprimatur
           Is theirs, and that no agitator
           Ought to persuade you to deny
           Their bombs and God and apple pie—
           An interlocked and cozy trinity—
           The very thing to wean you from
           Too much fine scrutiny of the bomb
           Or the fouled wells of your vicinity—
           Though their carcinogenic waste
           Is rather an acquired taste...."

11.18   If these seem feeble words as written,
They capture none of Liz's hold
On that packed courtroom. Phil sat smitten;
The pressmen scribbled notes; the old
Disgruntled judge (who just last Monday
Sentenced O'Hare) feared this was one day
His lawful victims might elude
The harvest of their turpitude.
The impassioned advocate was wearing
A cambric blouse, a wine-dark suit,
An air both fragile and acute—
And there was something in her bearing
That seemed to make her flame and burn
With sorrow, and with high concern.

11.19   After the courtroom celebrations,
Liz took her client out to lunch.
He said, "Thanks, Liz. Congratulations!
That was superb . . . but I've a hunch
That something's happened to upset you.
Don't bite your lip. Tell me. I'll let you
Speak without interruption, Liz;
I promise. Look, I'll bet it is
Something to do with John. . . ." Liz, crying
Through her mascara on her mousse,
Said, "Phil—it's over—it's no use—
I'll never marry him." Phil, sighing,
Said, "Are you sure?" Liz bent her head.
"Oh well then, Liz, try me instead."

11.20   Liz burst into astonished laughter.
Phil watched her with uncertain eyes.
She wiped her streaming tears, and after
A sneeze or two asked, "Is that wise?"
"Wise?" "Sure, Phil—we don't love each other!
To borrow wisdom from my mother,
It's love that makes the world go round!"
"That's bullshit!" grunted Phil. "I've found
That love's a pretty poor forecaster.
I loved a woman—and was dropped.
I loved a man—and that too flopped.
Passion's a prelude to disaster.
It's something else that makes me sure
Our bond can last five decades more.

11.21   There's lots of things I like about you:
Your guts and gumption, gait and girth. . . .
Oh, sure, I'd get along without you,
But, Liz, for what such things are worth,
We could be happy with each other."
Phil stopped, then added, "There's another
Reason as well: I'm certain Paul
Wouldn't object to you at all."
"Oh, is that so?" Liz smiled, "How flattering!
I'm unloved, but not quite blackballed.
A great proposal. I'm enthralled!"
"Oh, please, Liz, this suspense is shattering,"
Phil groaned, and paused for her to speak.
Liz laughed, "All right. First thing next week."

11.22   Phil started. "Liz, don't joke. I'm serious."
        "So am I, Phil—I like you too—
        You're stimulating, unimperious . . .
        What's more, you've opened up my view
        To the whole world. . . . And I'd far rather
        Marry a man who's a good father
        Than someone . . . I too don't feel sure
        I can trust passion any more. . . ."
        "But next week—Liz? Why, even sending
        Out cards takes time . . . and John? and Ed?"
        Liz quietly says, "What's dead is dead.
        Drawing things out to a heartrending
        Finis won't help. My mother's ill.
        The earlier the better, Phil."

11.23   Just as we find that the catalysis
        Of trauma or euphoria jerks
        Us into acts where fine analysis
        Could fling a frisbee in the works
        (How often, though, such rash transactions
        Prove happier than our prudent actions),
        Liz and Phil, too, together hurled,
        Flew forth to nest a snugger world.
        Liz's initial time span doubled,
        But two weeks later, man and wife
        Set sail on the calm pond of life.
        One quadrant of this, though, was troubled:
        Though Liz meant well, she seemed to act
        Toward John with rankling lack of tact.

11.24   John sat at home. The invitation
Liz sent him burnt his heart to frost.
As if he feared contamination
By something touched by her, he tossed
Her letter in the trash can, tearing
Into fine strips the gilt card bearing
The wedding date and winery crest
(R.S.V.P.); and half possessed
By disbelief, half by revulsion,
Shuddering to think two weeks had changed
Her smooth-faced love to mold, deranged
By cynical rage, scorn, and repulsion
In turn, with galvanizing hate
He wrote Liz a short note to state

11.25   (1) That he had received her letter;
(2) It had been destroyed unread;
(3)—And the earlier the better—
Liz should remove each clue and shred
Of paper, furniture, and clothing
That served to activate his loathing.
When she came round—she had the keys
To do the needful—it would please
John to be absent; through her mother
She could inform him of the date
She found convenient. He would wait
Her word on this; and (4) if other
Business remained, his lawyers would
Meet her, and clear things up for good.

11.26   John mails his letter; though it's petty
          (And though he well perceives this) he
          Can't keep from scattering black confetti
          —His hatred wilts his decency:
          His mouth is dry: his lacerated
          Welt-ridden ego's aggravated
          His will to bring grief on the heads
          Of the incipient newlyweds.
          So all her talk of love was spurious—
          He should have known she was the type
          To hook, then chuck him—her false hype—
          His credulous trust . . . John grows as furious
          At his gulled faith as at what he
          Sees as her suave duplicity.

11.27   Lost in a savage transportation
          Of grievance, he won't own that he
          Helped generate this new equation.
          Selective sensitivity
          To his ills, blindness to their feelings
          Of equal injury, his dealings
          With Phil and Liz to him seem just
          Reprisal for their breach of trust.
          Phil sends a note; John does not read it.
          "Some plausible and soothing froth,"
          He thinks, drunk on a bitter broth
          Of cynicism. "Well, I don't need it!"
          Lonely, and injured in his pride,
          His sorrow festers though denied.

11.28   None of his woes will lead to weeping.
He's not the type to cry—big boys
Don't cry—unless, with his will sleeping,
In dreams, at two at night, the ploys
Of recollection in a madness
Of uncontrol set free his sadness
Into his pillow; and his face
Grows taut next morning with disgrace—
With salt upon his cheeks, as shaming
As a wet dream—the spoor of tears
Insinuatingly appears
To pock his swindled features, maiming
His poise until, cologned and dressed,
He stares once more at Everest.

11.29   Work! Mighty projects need completion—
Mountains to flatten, seas to drain,
And bombs to build . . . Each day's accretion
Of labor settles on his pain
Its nacreous coat of insulation.
And if this trick of desperation
Is also madness of a kind
—More sleight of will than peace of mind—
At least it numbs him to the treachery
Of those he loved. . . . But love . . . John sighs,
And the thought hardens in his eyes
That any falsity or lechery
—If the heart's cold and stamped with scorn—
Can be indulged in, or be borne.

11.30   And so, with the accumulation
Of unindulgent days, combined
With the indulgent fermentation
Of one-night stands, John, now resigned
To loneliness, without compunction,
Flexes his charm in clean disjunction
From his sore heart, sifts bars each night
For "cute chicks," by next morning's light
Ejects the used and using stranger,
Shaves, dresses, drives to work, works, then,
As night falls, rakes the bars again
For a new conquést, free from danger,
In this athletic masque of lust,
Of trust or the demise of trust.

11.31   Had Liz left him, he'd have confided
In his best friend; or if estranged
From Phil, his lover could have guided
His lost heart homeward, and exchanged
His bitterness for understanding;
But now no current countermanding
The icy flow of his closed pain
Touches his coast. He thinks again
Of Janet, but since he's ignored her
These many months, is too ashamed
To call her; what's more, in his maimed
Misogyny, he can't afford her
Solicitude: for if she's kind
He would be forced to change his mind.

11.32   In San Francisco's snowless winter
The gray weeks rinse themselves away.
Liz thinks of John. A painful splinter,
Drawn in more deeply day by day
—Not of remorse so much, or fretful
Resentment, as of a regretful
Sense that when old friends fall apart
Things are not well—afflicts her heart.
John's note to her, harsh and censorious;
Phil's hand stretched out across the rift
Repelled outright; their New Year's gift
To John—a small, expiatorious
Italian alabaster dove
Mailed back without response, thanks, love,

11.33   Or (what did Liz expect?) civility—
All force on her what she's half known:
That, undermined in his virility,
John's pain-aversive life has grown
More loveless than before he met her.
No tenderness can gash or fetter
One who's seen through it all before.
Though void of hope, Liz makes one more
Attempt at reconciliation:
Her card, a single pleading line,
Arrives, ill timed, at Valentine.
This seals her excommunication;
John credits, almost with relief,
That Liz has tried to mock his grief.

11.34   Throughout the season, John, tormented
        By moods in turn depressed and foul,
        Soothes himself at the well-frequented
        Mixed singles bar, the Winking Owl.
        Whom should he meet one night that winter
        But Bjorn, the preening Swedish sprinter
        Who at John's housewarming had gazed
        Lasciviously at Rose, appraised
        Her coldly but in vain, and later
        Slickly seduced and lured to sleep
        Lucinda of the Liquid Sheep.
        From time to time he used to date her;
        At other times—and she knew this—
        He hungered for a change of bliss.

11.35   Tonight Bjorn tries to put the make on
        A dainty little doe-eyed lass.
        She proves no meager match to take on,
        Drinks up his drinks, fends off his pass
        ("So long, big boy!"), and leaves him stranded,
        Full-fraught with lust, but empty-handed.
        When round he casts his baleful eyes,
        Bjorn notices, to his surprise,
        John sitting in an alcove, talking
        To a lithe nymphet clad in red.
        Bjorn meditates, "And so to bed. . . .
        But why's John here?" And after stalking
        His doe to no effect, Bjorn walks
        Across to John, and grins, and talks.

11.36   Next day Bjorn mentions to Lucinda
He saw John at the Winking Owl.
The flame of rumor has struck tinder;
Lucinda lets out a sharp howl
Of mirth—and inside half an hour,
Thanks to the awesome branching power
Of Ma Bell's web, the fourth-hand news
Hits Jan, whom it does not amuse.
She talks to Sue, but Sue's no wiser.
Saddened as Jan is by the way
John's friendships have all gone astray,
She thinks, "Though I'm no temporizer,
It's best, for once, to wait and see.
He may not relish help from me."

11.37   Besides, it happens, she's so busy
Preparing for a summer show
In a small gallery, so dizzy
With sculpture, drink, and drums, that though
In slacker times she might have worried
About John more, her life's too hurried
For more than sympathy: the claims
Of cash flow and artistic flames
Have rendered her so incandescent
With inspiration (and with fear
As each month's ides of rent draw near)
That even Cuff and Link's incessant
High wauls, intense and Siamese,
Upon occasion, fail to please.

11.38   So though Jan suffers for him—really,
Why she still does is hard to say;
He's treated her less than ideally—
She can't divert an hour his way.
"It's just not possible," Jan's thinking. . . .
"Still, if I dropped in at the Winking
Owl, I suppose, to have a drink,
I might . . . in fact, I really think,
Tomorrow, since the band's not playing. . . ."
Somehow, in short, Jan finds the time.
John's absent when she enters. "I'm
A fool," she thinks. "Here I am, paying
Two dollars for a measly beer.
How do I know that he'll appear?"

11.39   He does. With startled recognition
He sees her face across the crowd.
Through Michael Jackson's taut rendition
Of "Beat It," shatteringly loud,
Jan tries to say, "Hey, how's it going?"
John frowns, walks over to her, slowing
Just once as a young woman's eyes
Rest on him with a smooth surmise.
"Who's that?" asks Jan. John shrugs his shoulders.
"Someone. Who knows? You like it here?
She's quite a babe! Another beer?
Night on the town, huh, Jan?' Jan smolders
At John's cool tone, but murmurs, "It's
My night off. Sure, I'll have a Schlitz."

11.40   As John surveys his singles heaven,
           Her heart is irked by his hard-boiled
           Slick patter: "... That one gets a seven....
           That's Martha: well-stacked but shop-soiled....
           Wow! Check the goods out on that cutie....
           But, heck, I'm failing in my duty—
           You're a newcomer here, and, Jan,
           I've got to help you get your man....
           You like that fellow? No—too hairy...
           —Of course, I'm not a judge—... or that
           Blond-haired dude? Hey, he's staring at
           You now, Jan—No, looks like a fairy...
           But curly hair turns on some chicks."
           Jan snaps: "And I'm turned off by hicks."

11.41   John's commentary halts. "But, baby,
           It's you who told me long ago
           To seize the day—remember?" "Maybe—
           But at the time I didn't know....
           And as for 'baby,' kindly can it.
           That turns me off as well. Just Janet—
           Got that?" She finishes her Schlitz:
           "... My God, this singles bar's the pits.
           I've got to get you out. I'm going
           To a café. You come as well...."
           What's on Jan's mind John cannot tell,
           But, revved for takeoff like a Boeing,
           She sweeps him up into the blue:
           Café Trieste, and tea for two.

11.42   So there they sit—and John is smiling,
           And Jan is not—and John says, "Jan?"
           And Jan thinks, "He's forever riling
           Me—why don't I dislike this man?
           Politically he's close to Nero.
           For tolerance he scores a zero
           Despite his catacombs of books.
           Am I just turned on by his looks? . . .
           At one time I was mad about him.
           Still, we broke up, and time's slipped by
           And I'm still here. In those days I
           Could hardly think of life without him.
           Poor Jan," she thinks, "I wish I could
           Have been there. I'd have done me good."

11.43   She laughs, and John looks up from sipping
           His tea and asks, "Well, what's the joke?"
           "Nothing," says Jan, "I was just slipping
           Back to our days of fire and smoke!"
           "Ah," John replies, and stares around him,
           Alarmed that she's about to sound him
           About his recent unsuccess.
           But Jan laughs, "We're both fools, I guess."
           Her voice—or something—has restored him
           To gentleness. "If I was rude,"
           He mutters, "blame it on my mood."
           She thinks: "I know why I adored him.
           Not for his looks . . . well, that's half true . . .
           It's simply that he loved me too."

11.44   She smiles again: "What a poor reason—
But—oh well—it will have to do."
Aloud she says, "John, it's the season
The whales swim down the coast. Do you
Want to drive up the Shoreline Highway
This Sunday afternoon? It's my way
Of simmering down when life is rough."
John says, "Well, my life's calm enough.
Admittedly, if I were wilting
With loneliness, Miss Nightingale,
Your panacea of a whale
Would suit me fine. But since my jilting
—Now that monogamy's removed—
I find my love life much improved."

11.45   Jan quietly slices through the specious
Fat of John's speech to his hard wound.
She says: "Look, John, don't be facetious.
You're wrong: it's not that I impugned
Your interactions with society
Or your amours in their variety.
I wanted you to come, that's all.
But don't decide now. Why not call
Me on the weekend?" ... Thus on Sunday
A picnic hamper packed for two,
Binoculars, sketch pad, corkscrew
And two files (to be read by Monday)
Usurp the rear of John's Peugeot
As northward to Muir Beach they go.

11.46   From the tall overlook, the indented
        Shoreline extends in cliffs and bays
        And promontories through the scented
        Wind-sheared sage northwest to Point Reyes.
        Northward, Mount Tamalpais lowers;
        Southward, through leather ferns, wildflowers
        —Tangling and twining through the lush
        Confusion of coyote brush
        And winter weeds—the blue Pacific,
        Unwrinkled as a pond, defines
        With wharves and cypresses and pines
        Three edges of the hieroglyphic
        Of San Francisco, still and square
        And sun-bleached in the ocean air.

11.47   Beyond the surf in smooth migration
        The great gray whales serenely go
        South from their summer habitation,
        The Arctic, down to Mexico.
        Swimming and surfacing, submerging
        Below the overlook, then verging
        The shore, they blow a trail of spouts
        Along their exodus. John shouts,
        "Hey, look! There's two—a calf and mother,
        Wouldn't you say?" Jan frowns: "Right here
        It's a bit early in the year
        For that, but maybe in another
        Couple of..." John says, "If we can,
        Let's meet again next Sunday, Jan."

11.48　　If Jan's surprised, she shows no inkling
　　　　　Of it at all. The rug is spread,
　　　　　The wine uncorked, and now they're sprinkling
　　　　　Salt on the eggs, and on the bread
　　　　　They pile cheese, lettuce, and salami
　　　　　Enough to satisfy an army.
　　　　　The sea breeze with its spice and bite
　　　　　Adds accent to their appetite.
　　　　　And when they've finished, Janet, leaning
　　　　　Against a pine tree, pen in hand,
　　　　　Sketches the precipice and sand,
　　　　　While John thinks, "Dammit—I've been meaning
　　　　　To read these files all day. How come
　　　　　I'm so relaxed my brain's gone numb?"

11.49　　Next weekend, gusts of squally weather
　　　　　Assail the coast, and they decide,
　　　　　Instead of driving north, to tether
　　　　　Their plans for Sunday to a ride
　　　　　On the bell-jangling locomotion
　　　　　Of city streetcars to the ocean.
　　　　　There they walk, hemmed in by the gray
　　　　　Residuum of a sunless day:
　　　　　The seethe of broken breakers sheeting
　　　　　Flat wastes of gray and glassy sand,
　　　　　And then, sucked seaward from the strand,
　　　　　A murky turquoise wash retreating,
　　　　　With half a hiss and half a sigh,
　　　　　West into mist and cloud and sky.

11.50   "God—what a day! God—how depressing!"
Says John: "Let's walk along the shore."
"Real yuck!" says Janet, acquiescing,
"Just for another hour more."
"Last Sunday it was crisp and sizzling,"
John mourns, "and now it's dank and drizzling."
Jan sighs, "We're bound to be wet through,
And then we'll both come down with flu..."
"...And die," adds John. "How disagreeable:
Drizzled to death, and in our prime—
With not a soul to care a dime...
But since our fate is quite foreseeable,
We're doomed, and might as well extend
This outing to its bitter end."

11.51   They stroll past driftwood, gnarled and whitened,
And braids of black where inlets pass
Into the sea, gray pebbles heightened
By green abraded gems of glass;
Large, yellow-beaked, orange-legged, fluffy
White gulls that strut among the scruffy
Plebeian pigeons by the pier;
Two parents yelling, "Shane, come here!
Come here this instant!"; frayed graffiti,
WHISKEY and MOM carved in the sand;
A collie splashing onto land,
Twig between teeth and an entreaty
—Once more, please!—written in his eyes;
Sand dollars, sandpipers, sand flies....

11.52   Jan sees a smooth, wave-worn sand dollar.
         "Intact!" she thinks, and rubs it clean.
         Far off somewhere the voices holler,
         "Shane! Shane! . . . Shane! Shane!" and in between
         The lunging water lifts and crashes
         Down on the sand and spills and thrashes,
         But Jan hears nothing as she stands,
         Looking at what lies in her hands:
         A cinquefoil perforated flower
         Pricked out upon a disk of white—
         Defectless emblem of delight
         And seal of oceanic power.
         She looks out seaward, unaware
         Of the mist moistening her black hair.

11.53   With open eyes, lost in reflection,
         Dreaming across the ocean, Jan
         Lets her mind trace its curved projection
         Beyond Hawaii to Japan,
         Envisioning her old grandmother
         In midlife journeying to another
         Language and continent and life,
         A pauper migrant's menial wife.
         With moral tags and bitter humor
         She built a fort against the ache
         Of exile for her husband's sake,
         And when he died, of a brain tumor
         In '43, lived thirty years
         Without complaint and without tears.

11.54   Jan looks around where John stands, facing
The static contours of the land.
"For the Atlantic!" Jan says, placing
The mystic circlet in his hand.
"Huh? A sand dollar," John smiles, turning
The object round: "A welcome earning:
Four sand quarters or ten sand dimes. . . ."
They walk on. Through the mist at times
The Cliff House looms, immense and sunless.
Offshore, from Seal Rock, through the dark
Chilled drizzle sea lions belch and bark,
And everything is foul and funless,
Unanimated, bland and bleak—
Except the Musée Mécanique.

11.55   Among its mirrors, pianolas,
Gumdrop machines, and biographs,
Refreshed by lukewarm Coca-Colas,
They pass an afternoon of laughs,
A rambling romp that only finishes
When, as the pallid light diminishes
Over the sea, Jan says, "I must
Go back now, John." John looks nonplussed.
Jan smiles, "I've got to earn my living. . . .
I've had a great time. Thanks a lot."
John, more surprised now, says, "For what?
My company?" With some misgiving
He goes on: "How about next week?"
Kissing her quickly on the cheek.

Twelve

12.1   John's nights are free, Jan's days. Their meetings,
       On weekend afternoons, are rare.
       And yet, the pattern of their greetings,
       The counted hours that they share,
       Drive him from his embittered brooding
       Against the cosmos—all, excluding
       His erstwhile friends. There, in his eyes,
       There is no balm of compromise,
       No herb of reconciliation.
       To talk of them, to speak their names
       Is to immerse him in the flames
       Of hatred, the intoxication
       Of a now long-fermented brew
       That burns his spirit through and through.

12.2   A waste, a puerile waste and pity,
Jan thinks, that these three former friends
Will not meet somewhere in the city
—Some neutral café—make amends
Or peace or mutual restitution,
Perform some ritual ablution
Of their ill will, and recognize
That life is short and that time flies,
Etcetera—and that, all things taken
Into account, John, Liz, and Phil
Have less of ill than of goodwill;
But when she mentions this, so shaken
Is she by John's extreme response,
She drops the matter—for the nonce.

12.3   When one considers how pain mangles
John, who believes he's duped by love,
When one considers that triangles
Such as the one described above
Lent five-star tragedy material
To Shakespeare and the Greeks, ethereal
Dream bubbles such as Janet blows
Of universal love expose
An aspiration somewhat artless
In one whose art's far from naive.
It's true that Jan does not believe
John's stance is reasonless or heartless;
She sees it, though, as rigid. Well,
Perhaps that's so; it's hard to tell.

12.4   Some claim the coast of California
Is seasonless, that there's no snow
To flavor winter. Others, born here
Or fleeing here—glad to forgo
The option of frostbitten fingers
And housebound months as hoarfrost lingers
Upon the firs, less picturesque
Than deadening, while from their desk
They'd stare past dark eaves fringed with icicles
Well into March, and scarcely dare
To breathe the east or midwest air—
Now yield, with tank tops, frisbees, bicycles,
Dogs, cats, and kids and tans and smiles
To spring's precocious warmth and wiles.

12.5   It's spring! Meticulous and fragrant
Pear blossoms bloom and blanch the trees,
While pink and ravishing and flagrant
Quince bursts in shameless colonies
On woody bushes, and the slender
Yellow oxalis, brief and tender,
Brilliant as mustard, sheets the ground,
And blue jays croak, and all around
Iris and daffodil are sprouting
With such assurance that the shy
Grape hyacinth escapes the eye,
And spathes of Easter lilies, flouting
Nomenclature, now effloresce
In white and lenten loveliness.

12.6   John views his disregarded garden
        Where flowers and weeds hold equal sway.
        He feels his resolution harden:
        "It's springtime, and it's Saturday.
        Jan is an excellent adviser.
        I ought to call her and apprise her
        That I need help in my attempt
        To keep my backyard couth and kempt."
        But when Jan comes, instead of dealing
        With mulch, mimosas, and manure
        They take a ride along the shore
        And, with a vernal verve of feeling,
        Talk of the past, of the old days
        Before they went their separate ways.

12.7   No wistfulness but, rather, laughter
        Tinges their speech. Do they refer
        To different beings? Even after
        She says to him and he to her
        That first love's best by definition
        They seem to state a proposition
        So distant from their lives that they
        Are quite untouched by it today.
        John lives each week, and takes things easy.
        Love's a mere word. Though it's a blast
        To screen old reels, the past's the past.
        If it intrudes, it makes him queasy.
        Singed once, he will not yield again
        Words that might cause him future pain.

12.8   But week by week, as springtime urges
      Him into the caressing sun,
      And the rain lessens, and March merges
      With April, and the benison
      Of days, their tread and their profusion,
      Distract his heart from its contusion,
      His visits to the bars decrease.
      If now and then he finds release
      From his aloneness with a stranger,
      His new companionship with Jan,
      Confined to daylight, helps him span
      The darkness safer from the danger
      Of the crude misery that drove
      Him into unknown arms for love.

12.9   One Tuesday night, the cancellation
      Of a performance frees the Sheep
      To savor the unique sedation
      Of soundlessness and early sleep.
      Jan turns her talents to creating
      Sushi and sashimi. While waiting
      For John (her guinea pig), she sets
      The chopsticks out, regales her pets
      With scraps of herring, then, abstracted,
      Turns to her sculpture, *Mother Hen*,
      Chisels away at it, and when
      The doorbell buzzes in protracted
      Protest, thinks, "Damn! Who can that be?
      Oh, John, of course! How dumb of me."

12.10　She yells a cheerful "I'm just coming,"
　　　　Runs down the stairs two at a time,
　　　　Hugs him, and with unconscious drumming
　　　　(Chisel on door), remarks, "John, I'm
　　　　Sorry, I'm in the very middle
　　　　Of . . . it's that hen . . . she's such a riddle. . . .
　　　　Go take a walk around the block
　　　　And come back here at eight o'clock."
　　　　John thinks, "She hasn't changed much, really,
　　　　In all these years." When he returns
　　　　They eat, and talk; and John's heart burns
　　　　With an old longing—is it merely
　　　　Night, or her unchanged waywardness?—
　　　　And he says, "Jan?" and she says, "Yes."

12.11　Tonight a quilt of peace surrounds him.
　　　　He dreams of nothing. He is free
　　　　Of all volition. It astounds him
　　　　How little now the enmity
　　　　Of the crass world, its fickle illness
　　　　Impinges on his crypt of stillness.
　　　　He sleeps, his cheek against her breast,
　　　　Unagitated, more at rest
　　　　Than when, the sensual excitement
　　　　Of strangers' lovemaking endured,
　　　　He flees to sleep with no accord
　　　　Between release and the indictment
　　　　His heart makes, that his love, hard sealed
　　　　With bitterness, rots unrevealed.

12.12   Yet, tender as is their lovemaking,
John gives his voice no leave to own
What his hand's touch, what his lip's quaking,
Unknown perhaps to him, has shown
More forthrightly than declaration;
And if Jan's heart knows the elation
It knew six years ago when they
Were lovers, she does not betray
By open word—for fear of sweeping
A turbid patina of dust
On the clean fabric of their trust—
That, as her heart was in his keeping
Once, and the sharer of his pain
And gladness, so it is again.

12.13   That Saturday the coaxing weather
Confetties the blue bay with sails.
John hires a small boat; together
They guide it out to watch the whales
For the last time this year, migrating
Northward again, and aggregating
In pods and pairs, but far from shore.
Though grocery shopping is a bore,
Tonight it almost seems a pleasure:
With friendly passion they discuss
The rival tastes of octopus
And squid, and how one ought to measure
The additives in bread and meat;
Then go to Jan's to cook and eat.

12.14   Next morning is spent bedbound, lazing—
        Until they hear the church clocks strike
        Eleven, while the cats, appraising
        The alien in Jan's bed, unlike
        Charlemagne or the Winery Persian,
        Display no vestige of aversion
        Towards it, glad to rub their furs
        Or butt their heads with fervent purrs
        Against the legs of Tutankhamen
        And John with equal nonchalance.
        At twelve they scratch the fridge, and dance.
        For John and Jan a bowl of ramen
        Capped with a raw egg serves for brunch,
        But Cuff and Link have squid for lunch.

12.15   And so the days pass. On occasion
        They see a Hitchcock matinee.
        At other times, at Jan's persuasion
        They go kitsch-hunting for the day.
        Jan manifests a greater relish
        The more ornate, bizarre, and hellish
        The objects she unearths: two pink
        Brass-gilded faucets for her sink,
        A Mickey Mouse phone and receiver....
        John looks shell-shocked, and cannot square
        (Of course, it's all her own affair,
        He thinks) a green ceramic beaver
        —Its teeth bared in a putrid smile—
        With Jan's own sober sculptural style.

12.16   Jan works long hours, tense, inspired.
         Ma Hen, her maiden work in stone,
         Is finished, and her brain is tired
         And her hand aches, and she's alone;
         But time's short now. She must make progress
         On *Biased Portrait of an Ogress*,
         The final sculpture for the show.
         With only fifteen days to go,
         "No time, no time, no time!' keeps dinning
         Into her ears. At last, two days
         Before the deadline, Janet says,
         "Oh God! A drink! It's done!" and grinning
         In gratified collapse, makes short
         Work of four glasses of white port.

12.17   Meanwhile, though John's received a bonus
         And a promotion, an unease
         Has seeped into his mind: the onus
         Of his work troubles him. He sees
         With a dark clarity, that either
         The bombs will fall or not, and neither
         Alternative gives cause for pride.
         If (a) they obsolesce inside
         Their silos, then his life's expended
         Creating something never used.
         Or else, if (b) ... but John's refused
         To assume this, and has long defended
         The assuring axiom that the more
         The bombs, the less the chance of war.

12.18   "Ah, well, my own work only deals with
         A minor part of what we do. . . .
         The silverware we eat our meals with
         Could wipe the human race out too. . . .
         And anyway, I've always reckoned—
         Better to die in one swift second
         Than with a bayonet in the crotch. . . ."
         He builds his case back, notch by notch.
         But when he adds, "Jan, these psychotic
         Peaceniks have no respect for law,"
         She quietly says, "My mother saw
         Her law-abiding, patriotic
         Father interned, by law. He died
         In '43, while still inside."

12.19   June tenth begins Jan's exhibition
         In a small gallery, Marcus Ladd,
         A revamped warehouse in the Mission.
         It looks good, and Jan's proud and glad—
         Till the art critic of *The Clarion*
         Flaps to the scene in search of carrion
         And glares in vulturine disgust
         At her live works. He writes: *I trust*
         Miss Hayakawa's terse aridity
         (Which she no doubt deems spare and fine)
         Does not mislead colleagues of mine
         (Though their vulgarian stupidity
         Rarely deserves such trust for long)
         To judge these feeble works as strong. . . .

12.20   *This exhibition, bland and themeless*
        —Bronzes and plasters, wood and stone—
        Promiscuously strung in schemeless
        Sequence strives vainly to disown
        Its formalism and immaturity.
        The great man's spoken. With security,
        The critics, free to take their cue
        From the first trump of his review,
        Now slither forth their own reviewing.
        These worms who, senile/trendy, hung
        Their hearts on soup cans and bat dung,
        Disparage Jan's exhibits, spewing:
        "Unsettled," "vacuous," "inbred,"
        "Cold," "marrowless," "unethnic," "dead."

12.21   Jan weeps in private with frustration.
        For all her courage she can't bear
        This universal condemnation.
        But she is lucky—in that where
        Others in such a situation
        Have turned away from their vocation
        With hurt and hopelessness and doubt,
        Her spirit will not flicker out.
        John's heart goes out to her, but really,
        In the sad hours that ensue
        There isn't much that he can do.
        She feels she's failed, and he can merely
        Hold her hand, frown, and iterate,
        "Your time will come, Jan. Just you wait."

12.22   In fact it's this that Jan, with laughter,
Repeats to those who sympathize
With her, or with her works—who (after
Reading *The Clarion* with bright eyes)
Quote in a sad voice, soft with gloating,
A phrase or two "that's just been floating
Around these days. . . . I might have read
It somewhere. . . ." But Jan feels half dead
Now that night's fallen, and she's climbing
The stairs. She gives the cats a kiss.
"John's right. I can't give in to this.
It's all a quirk of time—or timing—
Or something—Lord, do I feel beat!
Now what would you two like to eat?"

12.23   Next day Jan happens to be present
At Marcus Ladd when Liz and Phil
Come to look round. "Ah, what a pleasant
Surprise!" Jan shouts. Phil laughs: "Jan, will
You show us round yourself?" "Delighted!"
Liz says: "We read what that benighted
Creep of a *Clarion* critic wrote."
"Oh, him!" says Jan, and clears her throat:
"But, Liz, you look . . . Well, *are* you?" Flushing,
Liz says: "We haven't wasted time!
Paul's dubbed me Doubly Lovely. I'm
Now in my sixth month! Talk of rushing. . . ."
Jan smiles: "At eight this Friday night
I'm throwing a party. Come. All right?"

12.24   The party, planned to start at seven,
Once meant to mark the show's success,
Will act now as a wake to leaven
Its burial. Jan, through her distress,
Thinks, "It's a fine chance—what could match it?—
To force a burial of the hatchet....
It's good I asked them to come late.
I'll have John softened up by eight.
By nine they'll see their feud's a pity.
By ten, tears streaming from their eyes,
They'll pledge a love that never dies....
Now watch out, drive straight, Walter Mitty!"
Jan's let her fertile fancy goad
Her pickup halfway off the road.

12.25   This stalwart vehicle that's carried
Jan and her sculpture round for years,
Now rusty and, of late, much harried
By the complaints of age, appears
To be on its last legs (a metaphor
Hardly well-tuned), and not much better for
Checkups and oilings and repair,
It coughs and spasms now that a chair
And desk, with John's help, are transported
Up to his house: Jan's grandmom's old
Furniture which Jan isn't bold
Enough to risk to the assorted
Wine stains and cigarette burns and knocks
Of Friday night's prospective shocks.

12.26   On Friday morning, preparations
        Complete for that night's revels—rare
        Foresight for Jan, whose inclination
        Is to leave all such things to prayer—
        She drives to Stanford. Sue, who's leaving
        For France on Monday, has been grieving
        That, hassle-bound, she can't attend
        The celebration of her friend.
        So Jan drives down; and while assisting
        Sue in her packing, sheds a tear
        That she won't see her for a year,
        And Sue too, twisting and untwisting
        Her hands, is silent as they part. . . .
        But now Jan's pickup will not start.

12.27   No coaxing, gear manipulation,
        Or bluster has the least effect.
        At last Jan in exasperation
        Says, "Well, I guess I should inspect
        The bus and train timetables. Let me
        Work this thing out, or it'll get me
        Into real trouble. John can hold
        The fort—but since I haven't told
        Him they'll be there, I'd better call them
        And ask them to come later still.
        Yes, that way I'll be sure I will
        Be home to see John doesn't bawl them
        Out of the house. . . . What's Liz's new
        Number up in the city, Sue?"

12.28   Jan phones; Phil makes a fresh suggestion:
        "Jan, I phoned Matt Lamont today.
        Since he's my doc, I had a question
        About Liz.... Fine! ... Well, anyway,
        Matt said in passing he'd be coming
        Northward today. How about bumming
        A ride up with him. Here's his phone....
        He's taking off some time with Joan
        And Chuck; the three of them are going
        For two weeks—up to Oregon....
        Oh, if you really want some fun,
        Ask how his orchids have been growing....
        Eight-thirty then, Jan? ... Yes, that's right.
        Better call soon. See you tonight."

12.29   Jan phones, walks over. "It's no trouble
        At all," says Matt. "Meet my wife, Joan.
        And this is Chuck.... Excuse the rubble—
        It's a rock garden. We've not grown
        Cacti before—it's quite exciting—
        We hope, by next year.... Now, stop fighting
        With Mom.... Joan, dear, it's getting late...."
        Matt breaks off here to arbitrate
        Between them on the question whether
        Chuck's *Star Wars* weaponry should go
        With them to Oregon—and so,
        When in an hour they're all together
        (Appeased, prepared, and locked and packed)
        Inside the car, and the car's backed

12.30   Out of the driveway, it is getting
Darker, and Jan now fears she's late.
The moon is thin. The sun is setting.
She glances at her watch: "It's eight.
I won't be there in time to screen them
From any sparks that fly between them."
She thinks, "Please, John, don't be a fool.
I love you. Please don't lose your cool."
The radio's tuned to a jazz station;
Chuck, in the back, is half asleep
On Joan's arm; Jan tries hard to keep
Her mind, meanwhile, on Matt's damnation
Of legislators who betray
Bird sanctuaries along the bay.

12.31   Joan laughs, "Now, Jan, don't let Matt bore you!
Don't listen to him with such deep
Attention, or he'll fall flat for you....
Sweetheart, it seems Chuck's gone to sleep....
You know, Jan, as a rule, Matt's never
So voluble—I haven't ever
Seen it before—with someone he's
Just met.... Well, darling, shall we seize
Janet and take her with us?..." Slowly,
Dusk turns to dark, and from the car
Jan sees how, star by star by star,
The sky, now constellated wholly,
Domes over the fluid freeway, bright
With red and silver lanes of light.

12.32   Back in her studio, John's perplexity
        Increases as the minutes pass.
        He makes sure that the chilled convexity
        Of everybody's champagne glass
        Is smoothly brimmed; but all his suavity
        Fails to disguise his heart's concavity.
        "Where's Jan?" he thinks, half sad, half cross.
        "She's always late. I'm at a loss
        To talk to any of these arty
        Weirdos and freaks. . . . Oh, oh, there's Bjorn,
        Courting that Sheep with crumpled horn. . . .
        Dammit, where's Jan? This is her party!"
        His ponderings abruptly freeze
        As, turning to the door, he sees

12.33   —O God! How could Jan do this to him?
        To leave him no excuse for flight
        Or subterfuge, to superglue him
        To the host's chair, then to invite—
        Liz and Phil here? As pale as paper,
        As if he'd just inhaled the vapor
        Of Love Canal, face white with strain,
        John pours two glasses of champagne,
        Then, walking to the door and handing
        Them to the guests—a gesture planned
        So as not to have to take their hand—
        Mutters, "In here—or on the landing—
        Enjoy yourselves. As you can see,
        I've got my work cut out for me."

12.34 He turns around abruptly, leaving
       Liz and Phil chilled. Liz wants to flee
       This bitter vision. Phil, retrieving
       A tinge of equanimity,
       Says, "Liz, let's speak to Jan," then, seeing
       Jan isn't there, thinks, "Is she being
       Deliberately elusive? Or
       Didn't she get a ride? I'm sure
       Matt hadn't left yet when I told her
       To call him." He goes up to John
       And asks him, "John, where's Janet gone?"
       "Not here yet." John's eyes flash and smolder.
       "Well, may I use the phone?" "Feel free,"
       John says with tight civility.

12.35 Phil dials the Lamonts'. Arriving
       At the conclusion that they've gone,
       He tells John: "The Lamonts were driving
       This evening up to Oregon.
       Jan got a ride with them. I'm guessing
       Friday night traffic is what's messing
       Their timing up. An hour more,
       And Jan will be here, that's for sure."
       John thinks, "I'm not so sure about it.
       It's quite a standard Janet jape
       To set things up, and then escape.
       But Oregon? Sure, I don't doubt it. . . .
       Damn, damn that woman and her wiles—"
       And then, despite himself, he smiles.

12.36   Jan's absent, but her party's swinging.
Funny that no one seems to care,
John muses (now the phone is ringing)
Whether or not the host is there.
He squeezes through the reveling fever
Toward the phone, lifts the receiver:
"Yes ... Hayakawa ... What? Police? ..."
All sounds around him swiftly cease.
Phil looks at John: eyes closed, and gasping
As if for life and breath, he stands,
The Mickey Mouse phone in his hands,
Reiterating without grasping
Three words that gradually sink in
As he repeats them: "Next of kin?"

Thirteen

13.1   A month has passed. The moon is rising.
A balmy night in late July
Rests on the city, exorcising
The summer fog. Around the sky
The great imputed constellations,
Differently seen by different nations,
And that great current over all
That Janet's grandmother would call
The Silver River, faintly glowing,
Counter the city's glittering grid.
The Transamerica Pyramid
Spears up in light. A breeze is flowing
(Quite as love that's left unsaid)
Through the straight streets. And Jan is dead.

13.2 And Matt. And Joan. The one survivor,
   Saved when Joan flung herself across
   His body, is Chuck. The other driver
   —A high school kid—was at a loss
   When he came to: "I didn't mean it,"
   He sobbed. "If only I had seen it!"
   Though bruised, and limp as a rag doll
   With shock, remorse, and alcohol,
   He was unharmed. A trial ended
   The term of his repentance; here
   He pleaded guilty. For a year
   His license is to be suspended.
   The dead are dead; and why destroy
   The youth—the judge thought—of a boy?

13.3 A month has passed. Chuck is now staying
   With Liz and Phil. His broken arm
   Is healing. Cuff and Link are playing
   With Charlemagne. No serious harm
   Has come to Liz—the shock bypassed her;
   Phil, shielding her from the disaster,
   Dealt with the details of the late
   Matthew and Joan Lamont's estate.
   Again tonight the moon advances,
   A casual crescent, fine and high,
   A sort of innocent passerby
   Across the city of Saint Francis,
   Across the freeway, red and white,
   With last month's curvature and light.

13.4   Patron of your beloved city,
       O San Francisco, saint of love,
       Co-sufferer in searing pity
       Of all our griefs, whom from above
       Birds would alight on, singing, feeding
       Within your hands—hands pierced and bleeding
       With Christ's own signs—who, stigmatized
       As dupe and clown, apostrophized
       The sun in its white blistering starkness
       As brother, and the blistered moon
       As sister, and who, blind at noon,
       Opened your heart and sang in darkness—
       And where it was, sowed light, look down.
       Solace the sorrows of your town.

13.5   Phil, more distressed by the calamity
       Than he himself shows, sometimes sees
       His son and Chuck, in quiet amity,
       Playing—and Chuck abruptly freeze
       And—gasping, sobbing, wheezing, crying—
       Relive again his mother's dying:
       The blood, the broken sleep, the scream:
       Was that, or is this now, a dream?
       One day Phil, shattered by his pleading
       To "take me back home," drives him down
       To his old house. The grass is brown
       In patches, and the flowers want weeding;
       But brilliant in their summer bloom
       Geraniums mass outside Chuck's room.

13.6   The boy stands there, pulls off a petal,
        Sniffs it, and frowns, then tries the door;
        Touches the monogram of metal
        His father cast the year before;
        Reads, 'M,J,C,' and stands there silent;
        Then with a sudden rage, a violent
        Plea in his voice, shouts, "Let me in.
        It's my house—and I live here." Thin
        Hysteria seizes him. Phil, stroking
        The boy's head, says, "Sure, Chuck, sure, sure . . .
        Here we are." Chuck bolts through the door
        And shouting in a voice half choking
        With fear and dust, "Mom! Mom! Dad! Dad!"
        Runs through the rooms as if he's mad.

13.7   "It's me—it's me—Chuck. Mom! Dad!" Stumbling
        With tears that blind him, Chuck falls down
        And hurts his other arm. Phil, mumbling,
        "Oh, Chuck! Oh no!" drives through the town
        To Mrs. Craven's for assistance.
        Chuck, silent now, shows no resistance
        As Mrs. Craven laughs, "So, Chuck!
        Looks like you're really out of luck:
        Both parents—now both arms!" and, tying
        A bandage, says, "Now for some fun. . . .
        A doctor's wife and doctor's son
        Should make great partners. Let's go flying! . . .
        Sure, he'll be safe. I've learned to fly. . . .
        Sure—here's my license: twelfth July!"

13.8   Phil smiles at her with resignation:
      "Ah, Mrs. Craven, now we've gone,
      Who's here to save you from temptation?
      You'll be in space next." "Well, for one—
      Rowena! Since she's been elected
      To City Hall, as a respected
      Councilor, she feels bound to see
      Her mother acts judiciously."
      Phil laughs, "Well, well! Congratulations!
      What happened to her quilts? Her van?
      Her Grand Quest for the Perfect Man?"
      "All gone! These days it's perorations
      On public spending, property tax,
      And programs that deserve the ax. . . ."

13.9   Sitting in the small Cessna, flying
      Along the algae-tinted shore
      Of the long bay, Chuck squints down, trying
      To make his house out. Then with awe
      He points: "That's it back there. I see it—
      With the red flowers. That must be it,"
      And laughs out loud with sudden joy.
      When Mrs. Craven gives the boy
      A hug, he once again grows quiet.
      She says, "Look, Chuck, life's tough! When you
      Are lonely, or just feeling blue,
      Come over—we two'll stage a riot.
      How does that sound?" Chuck, somewhat bleak,
      Replies, "I might be blue next week."

13.10   Are the dead, too, defiled by sorrow,
Remorse, or anguish? We who live
Clutch at our porous myths to borrow
Belief to ease us, to forgive
Those who by dying have bereft us
Of themselves, of ourselves, and left us
Prey to this spirit-baffling pain.
The countries round our lives maintain
No memoirists and no recorders.
Those who are born are too young, those
Who die too silent, to disclose
What lies across the occluded borders
Of this bright tract, where we can see
Each other evanescently.

13.11   The night John heard that Jan was dying,
Trembling, and dazed with grief, he drove
To the hospital where she was lying,
Sunk in a coma. When he strove
To induce the starched and startled nurses
With incoherent tears and curses
(—Since he was not her next of kin
And looked half crazed, to let him in
Seemed rash to them—) merely to let him
Say just one word to her, just one . . .
They told him it could not be done
Until their supervisor met him.
"She'll be down soon," they sighed, and fled.
She came. But Jan by then was dead.

13.12   It was the weekend. Numb with sorrow
John sat at home, lost in the thought
That if she'd been alive, tomorrow
They'd planned a trip.... In fact he ought
To get the picnic hamper ready
And phone Jan.... With a dim, unsteady
Terror of fact, his deepening grief
Shook from belief to disbelief.
The unforgiving realization
Of his own love now pierced his heart
So savagely and wrenched apart
His spirit with such desperation,
He felt he never would regain
The fervor to outlive this pain.

13.13   In those first days, a taut emotion
Of guilt and panic seized his heart.
The vehement delusive notion
That somehow he had played a part
In Janet's death, and was ineligible
To share her dying, grew intelligible
To his despair-demented brain.
Helpless to stem or to restrain
The tears that were forever starting
For no immediate cause at all,
Afraid, and avid, to recall
Their every meeting, every parting,
His first sight of her face, his last,
He sank his life into the past.

13.14　As if some random psychedelic
　　　　Drunkard or lunatic or child
　　　　Had left a daubed and reckless relic
　　　　On his mind's walls, with bright and wild
　　　　And unaccountable lucidity
　　　　—So forcible in their vividity
　　　　That his perceptions seemed unhinged—
　　　　Old images of Jan impinged
　　　　On his dimmed life. At work, or driving
　　　　To work, or after work, at home,
　　　　She seemed to be with him, to come
　　　　To him (thus brokenly surviving)
　　　　Like a rich revenant of life—
　　　　Seizing a chisel or a knife,

13.15　Or standing in the doorway, looking
　　　　At him with an ironic smile
　　　　When he, for once, was late; or cooking
　　　　Some dish he dared not say was vile
　　　　For fear she'd angrily ignore him
　　　　Or instigate the cats to claw him
　　　　Or light an anxious cigarette. . . .
　　　　It seemed to him that to forget
　　　　Her for a minute, for an hour
　　　　To be without her, was a fate
　　　　More painful than this pain—a state,
　　　　Besides, so much beyond his power,
　　　　The thought seemed as dismissive of
　　　　His sanity, as of his love.

13.16   Some days, it seemed, the analgetic
Monotony of work relieved
His heart. His boss was sympathetic;
But though he saw John was bereaved
And felt for him, his air of curtness
And John's own deepening inertness,
Distance, and apathy deterred
Much speech. And now, the work that blurred
The edges of his pain, constraining
His thoughts for eight hours of the day
To griefless objects, in a way
Appeared to him a kind of feigning,
A fraud which, while it brought relief,
Itself, at one remove, dealt grief.

13.17   Sometimes his unassuaged obsession
To find some pattern in, some cure
For Jan's death, led to an expression
Of prayer—less to reassure
His heart with hope or superstition
Than, with quotidian attrition,
To abrade its pointlessness and pain—
Yet what could he expect to gain
(He wondered) scouring thus for reasons
For one terrestrial incident
A universe as innocent
Of the night sky, the altering seasons,
And human passion as of steel,
Alcohol, or a steering wheel?

13.18   By day the city shines, and nightly
Glows with the stars. A month goes by.
The crescent moon, slimly and whitely,
Rests in the lenient evening sky.
In Golden Gate Park, John is walking.
Near him, he hears a couple talking:
"Well, I don't really want a ring."
"Why not?" "It's kind of threatening.
I'd think of you without volition,
Not just at times when I decide!"
They laugh.... John thinks, since Janet died,
For him, at least, there's no decision,
When every day in every place
He's haunted by her eyes, her face,

13.19   Even her voice.... He fears he's going
Crazy.... He sometimes hears her say
His name ... not when the day is flowing
Out with the tide, when twilight may
Extend its mist of imprecision
Beyond the premises of vision,
But in bright daylight, sane and clear,
He hears what no one seems to hear.
The bustle of the cafeteria
Continues; and his boss goes on
Talking, deaf to her voice, and John,
Cut off from him by a hysteria
That soaks through him like a high tide,
Sets down his fork, and walks outside.

13.20   Or late at night—when after turning
        The lights out, he's in bed alone,
        He hears her voice, and waves of yearning
        Drench his taut body to the bone,
        And a sick turmoil of desire
        Stirs through him with a craving fire
        For her, her hand to touch his hair,
        Her indrawn breath, and everywhere
        The unique musk of excitation
        Her body breathed when they made love.
        Each night, like dreams, strange figments of
        Their nights recur, prefiguration
        Of dreams themselves. One night he dreamed
        He stood by the seashore. It seemed

13.21   A woman with white hair was standing,
        Her back to him, before a grave.
        The other mourners were disbanding.
        She alone stood there still. A wave
        Of pity and incomprehension
        Swept over him. With close attention
        He saw her knotted fingers, pale
        With age, her body stooped and frail,
        Her head bent, as if she were weeping.
        He could not see her face or tell
        Whose grave it was. A streetcar bell
        Disturbed the air; and he was sleeping
        In a dark room, and Jan was there,
        Her gnarled hand on his silver hair.

13.22   He woke; as if a grip were choking
        The life from him, gasping for breath,
        He flailed and wept. Such dreams, evoking
        The present vision of his death,
        Random and steep, without cessation,
        Half terror and half consolation,
        Infect his nights; and through his days
        The pressure of his longing plays
        Tricks with his eyes. He sees her buying
        A yellow rose, a bunch of ferns
        From a street vendor. When she turns,
        A stranger's face observes him crying.
        He tries to speak, but his dismay
        Constricts him. Irked, she turns away.

13.23   The knowledge that he never mentioned
        His love for her, or heard her say
        That she loved him—his well-intentioned
        Design to keep all pain at bay,
        To shield him from the agitation
        Of passion with the insulation
        Of casual conduct, light and bland—
        Hurts like a nail torn from his hand.
        She died alone, with no one near her.
        Wretched to think he could not go
        Into her room, he feels that though
        She could not hear him, or he hear her,
        If somehow he had said a word
        Of love, she would have somehow heard.

13.24   Weak with uncertainty and bitten
        By suppurating pain and love,
        Yearning for some small proof, some written
        Message from her, not thinking of
        How he can bring himself to do it,
        He sits at Jan's old desk, goes through it
        Drawer by drawer, page by page
        —Old bills, old letters—to assuage
        His thirst for some clue, some solution—
        And there, with his old letters, sees
        The note he wrote to Anne T. Friese
        Inviting her (in his locution)
        "To dinner following a play
        If you are free next Saturday."

13.25   He looks at it. The sweet persuasion
        Of longing says: Take this as proof
        She loved you, saw through your evasion
        And knew your love, was not aloof
        From you; and without pride or rancor
        Kept all you gave her. Do not hanker
        For clarity; you cannot find
        It now, or ever; be as kind,
        As generous, and as incisive
        With your grief as you know she'd be.
        She loved you undeludedly
        Though—self-protectively derisive
        Of love, deluded and self-maimed
        (Or unillusioned, as you claimed)—

13.26   You gave her nothing.... John sits, staring
         At the old desk with thoughts like these,
         Too self-reproachful, with no bearing
         On his slight note to Anne T. Friese—
         More, it would seem, on the grief gnawing
         His mind as, day by day, withdrawing
         From every thought but those that bring
         Her life to life, he tries to wring
         Meaning from things that have no meaning,
         And scrapes at rusted words that yield
         Few glints of insight. The dark field
         Has little gold for all his gleaning.
         He haunts the past, but with no gain
         Of certainty to ease his pain.

13.27   Meanwhile the papers, true to fashion,
         Whose candid columns overspill
         With delicacy and compassion,
         Sniff out, with truffle-hunting skill,
         A local human-interest story:
         Young Artist Mown Down in Her Glory;
         And press Jan's parents, as they reel
         With private anguish, to reveal
         Relics of their distinguished daughter—
         For now the critics, Janus-faced,
         And those with wealth and time and Taste,
         Scavengers at a scene of slaughter,
         Flock to her show; and Marcus Ladd
         Pulls off the greatest coup it's had.

13.28   The brassy *Clarion*, as appalling
        In its lickspittling of the dead
        As in its comprehensive mauling
        Of what was young, and lived and bled,
        Issues an article deploring
        Those who found Janet's sculpture boring.
        Enticed by her postmortem rise
        The journal scurries to revise
        Its judgment: *What some call aridity*
        In Hayakawa's work (and there
        Are untrained eyes that deem it bare),
        Seen rightly, is a tense fluidity,
        A classic leanness that at length
        Will be applauded for its strength....

13.29   *Such startling sureness and maturity*
        And sense of form for one so young
        (Which braved long years of sad obscurity
        And the crude taunts detractors flung)
        Leave us no doubt that Hayakawa
        Will rank with Moore and Kurosawa,
        Or even—this is hard to gauge—
        With Pollock, Ashbery, and Cage.
        With the same zeal with which they pulped her
        (But with a new tune: "It's too bad—
        Indeed, insulting—Marcus Ladd
        Hardly befits a major sculptor"),
        The critics, like a scabrous scurf,
        Now dandruff back upon their turf.

13.30   Would it have given Jan some pleasure,
      This fat—albeit fickle—praise?
      Would she have looked at it at leisure,
      Stood at the mirror, tried a phrase—
      "Too big ... too baggy ... too belated,
      But just the boost for which I've waited;
      Perhaps I'll land a grant at last!"
      Or would such flatulent bombast
      From such a source have made her scornful
      Of her own work? Or turned her head?
      Or left her cold? Since Jan is dead—
      Survived by nothing but two mournful
      Cats, and her parents, and the stray
      Thoughts of a few friends—who can say?

13.31   The city's resting in late summer
      Beneath its foggy pleasure dome;
      And Liquid Sheep have a new drummer;
      And Cuff and Link have a new home.
      September nears; and Cuff is leaping
      Onto the chair where Link is keeping
      A fierce lookout for Chuck and Paul—
      Who on their cream furs shaved a scrawl,
      A ragged C or L, a marker
      To help distinguish them—a bold
      Brown glyph: where shaved and therefore cold,
      A Siamese's hair grows darker.
      Poor Cuff and Link find meager peace
      From Chuck's assaults and Paul's caprice.

13.32 While the frenetic foursome tussle,
       The embattled adults strive to keep
       A zone of refuge in the bustle:
       Charlemagne's curled up, half asleep,
       On the piano, where Phil's sitting,
       And Liz hums tunelessly while knitting. . . .
       Thus the young yahoos coexist
       With whoso list to list to Liszt. . . .
       Phil thinks: "It's so abrupt, it's numbing.
       Last August, it was Paul and me—
       And now it's two, plus two, plus three:
       Seven! and soon an eighth is coming. . . .
       Hope it's a girl. It would be good
       For the boys too. . . . Perhaps I should

13.33 Tell them to stop the racket. Oh well,
       Liz doesn't seem to mind. It's great
       That she and Paul have got on so well!
       And Chuck's learned chess too. . . . We'll vacate
       This place soon; maybe in November;
       It's fine for four, but . . . I remember,
       When Paul was born, Claire and I thought
       Our house too small. . . . Why have I brought
       Claire into this? Liz looks so happy—
       Unlike in spring, when she was sick.
       That yoga's really done the trick. . . .
       And even Charlemagne's less scrappy
       Since Cuff and Link moved in. That's strange . . .
       I thought cats . . . odd how things can change.

13.34 —And do change.... As for Chuck, poor fellow,
    I can't tell if he likes it here.
    Still, Mrs. Craven seems to mellow
    Him down a bit. But if, last year,
    Someone had told me she'd quit smoking
    I'd bet my life that he was joking.
    Of course, if someone said she'd fly
    I'd do the same.... I wonder why
    Matt left that note about adoption
    —It's kind of eerie—in his will:
    If we both die, we hope that Phil....
    Of course we'll want to take the option.
    Things may be tight; but if we must,
    I'm sure we could apply Chuck's trust....

13.35 I only wish Liz weren't so worried
    About her mother. I suspect
    That's the main reason why she's hurried
    Into all this. But why dissect
    Our happiness? It's self-defeating...
    Like all this chocolate she's been eating:
    'It makes no difference, now I'm fat—
    I want an It's-It, and that's that!'
    Well, one month more.... I wonder, after
    The baby's born, if Mom will deign
    To visit—and at least refrain
    From mentioning Claire. I'd like to draft her
    Into the baby-care routine.
    Most grandmothers enjoy that scene...."

13.36   "So little time!" Phil thinks; the extended
        Household, and the Lamonts' estate,
        And his new part-time job have ended
        That sedentary if not sedate
        Era of talk and contemplation,
        Whose slow-maturing culmination,
        The Lungless March throve on the zest
        And leisure those like Phil possessed. . . .
        He looks with envious admiration
        At the immobile Charlemagne,
        The quondam scourge of Liz's reign,
        Survey the room from his high station,
        Retired, at last, by bent and right
        Her beadsman now, who was her knight.

13.37   So little time. . . . Now Liz's mother
        Puts her affairs in order, tends
        Her pain, and by one means or other,
        Contrives to meet her various friends.
        The family drives up to Sonoma
        Each week; each week the fused aroma
        Of dust and diesel, leaf and grape,
        Imbues the reddening landscape.
        While Paul and Chuck run round at leisure
        And speculate, "I bet she dies
        Before the baby's born!" she cries
        At the inimitable pleasure
        Of seeing the young ruffians play
        Out in the vineyard, far away.

13.38   There is no hope now of remission.
Her looks betray the suffering borne
With every passing week's attrition.
Liz soothes her father as, heart torn,
He does his rounds of vineyard duty:
"Ah, Liz, your mother was a beauty—
And still is, if the truth be told.
We thought we two might have grown old
Together. . . . What makes this so crazy
Is that she's only fifty-five. . . ."
Liz thinks, "Please, God, keep her alive
Another month. . . ." Toward the hazy
Horizoned dust they slowly walk,
Sharing the lapsing balm of talk.

13.39   While Paul is mocking Liz's waddle
To Chuck's enraptured shouts and hoots,
And both together try to swaddle
The Winery Cat, a car horn toots.
The car halts; out step beast and bwana.
Ed walks inside, while the iguana,
Tied to a nearby redwood tree,
Drops its slow head, and clammily
Observes the amber sunshine falling
Upon the graystone winery. . . . .
A fat, enamored bumblebee
Chases the Winery Cat, who's hauling
A mauled and trembling mouse indoors
To Chuck and Paul's amazed applause.

13.40   Schwarz sees the duo, and starts hissing. . . .
        Inside the house, the tearful Ed
        Is saying something as he's kissing
        His mother's cheek; she lies in bed;
        The window's open, and the fragrant
        Late summer scents, the sweet and vagrant
        Calls of a mockingbird lilt through;
        She sits up, looks out at the view.
        Now they're discussing Ed's vocation.
        Ed says: "No, Mom, not yet. I may
        Find someone who can point the way
        Or wait, perhaps, for inspiration.
        I don't know. I'll decide . . . next year."
        She smiles: "Now don't look sad, Ed, dear."

13.41   Ed says: "Mom, let me write a letter
        To Sue. . . ." His mother says: "Now wait;
        Listen to me. I think it's better
        To leave things as they are. I'd hate
        To have her leave France and come flying
        All the way home to see me dying.
        Everyone knows the thing has spread,
        But who can tell when I'll be dead?
        If I hang on for six months after
        Sue flies back, must the poor girl stay
        And suffer while I waste away?
        Not on my life, Ed!"—and with laughter
        Not wholly free, yet not untrue,
        She adds, "I'd do the same with you."

13.42   Dinner is strained tonight. Ed's father
       Suggests Ed work at the vineyard
       Next year. But Ed replies, "I'd rather
       Follow my own nose, Dad...." (They've sparred
       About this in the past, though lately
       His father's arguments have greatly
       Increased in frequency and thrust.)
       Ed turns to Liz and Phil. "... I must
       Tell you this—though you won't believe me....
       Last evening—you know how well-dressed
       John is—I've always been impressed—
       I saw—the light did not deceive me—
       John, in a crumpled suit, unshaved,
       Walking on Market.... When I waved,

13.43   He kind of stared, then recognized me—
       And then—just sort of slunk away.
       He looked real—sleazy. It surprised me...."
       Phil stares at Ed in sharp dismay.
       Liz puts her arm round Phil—"Love, shouldn't
       We try to find ... I mean, why couldn't
       We write his father? He's in Kent—
       I could find out—and if we sent...."
       Phil says, "Liz, don't get agitated.
       It really isn't good for you.
       If there was something we could do....
       The fact is, he's so isolated
       By all this pain and bitterness.
       There's not much we can do, I guess...."

13.44   When dinner's done, the two boys bully
         Their "Uncle Ed" (a name he hates)
         Into a game of chess. When fully
         Engulfed by foemen, Ed stalemates
         The battle by a machination
         That wins extreme disapprobation
         From Paul, who claims it "isn't fair."
         Ed laughs, and gets up from his chair.
         "Have, by the way, you two decided
         What the new baby's going to be?"
         "A boy," Paul says assuredly.
         "Bet not," says Chuck, who's always prided
         Himself on thinking such things through:
         "Bet you a dollar." "Bet you two!"

13.45   The baby's born in late September:
         A bald and podgy nine-pound boy.
         The household greets its latest member
         With vast jocosity and joy.
         At the bewildered Cobb & Kearny
         Liz hands cigars to each attorney,
         Then takes six months maternity leave.
         Chuck's lost two bets, but does not grieve.
         The baby weaves his web of magic:
         The three wise cats admire his crib;
         Phil says, "He's beautiful!" (a fib);
         And Liz, no longer polyphagic
         And bulbous, now attempts once more
         Habiliments that she once wore.

13.46   Why all this madness over babies?
　　　　　—And how come even Mrs. Weiss,
　　　　　Who spurned Liz as if she had rabies,
　　　　　Agrees abruptly to be nice;
　　　　　What's more, consents to come and visit!
　　　　　Is it their helplessness? What is it?
　　　　　These idiots with insistent ids
　　　　　Who yowl when their unbridled bids
　　　　　For love or milk go unregarded
　　　　　For seven seconds—or who bawl
　　　　　For no substantial cause at all—
　　　　　Why are these egotists bombarded
　　　　　With kisses, hugs, and smiles to spare?
　　　　　Others, I think, deserve a share.

13.47   How ugly babies are! How heedless
　　　　　Of all else than their bulging selves—
　　　　　Like sumo wrestlers, plush with needless
　　　　　Kneadable flesh—like mutant elves,
　　　　　Plump and vindictively nocturnal,
　　　　　With lungs determined and infernal
　　　　　(A pity that the blubbering blobs
　　　　　Come unequipped with volume knobs),
　　　　　And so intrinsically conservative,
　　　　　A change of breast will make them squall
　　　　　With no restraint or qualm at all.
　　　　　Some think them cuddly, cute, and curvative.
　　　　　Keep them, I say. Good luck to you;
　　　　　No doubt you used to be one too.

13.48　　Marie Dorati is in raptures
　　　　About her flesh-and-blood grandchild.
　　　　"Look at that nose, Mike—it recaptures
　　　　My father's nose. Look, look, he smiled. . . .
　　　　Oh, what a darling—what a beauty—
　　　　What name have you . . . oh, what a cutie!. . . .
　　　　What name have you decided on?"
　　　　Liz says: "We think we'll call him John."
　　　　John Weiss looks troubled, then starts crying.
　　　　Phil picks him up, and calms him down.
　　　　He gurgles, and Liz laughs, "You clown!"
　　　　Then rocks him gently, hushabying
　　　　Him off to slumber, while Marie
　　　　Leans on her pillows painfully.

13.49　　She is near death; and one week later
　　　　No longer suffers any pain.
　　　　No cancer now can macerate her.
　　　　Immune to the October rain
　　　　That twinged her bones, her ashes mingle
　　　　With vineyard earth till not a single
　　　　Mark of her being signifies
　　　　A spot where something of her lies.
　　　　She dies in the mid-harvest season.
　　　　The crush is on, and nothing yields
　　　　To the imperative of the fields:
　　　　Mike works on; no one thinks it treason;
　　　　They know the vines grant no reprieve.
　　　　He grieves, but with no time to grieve.

13.50   Days pass, and on the golden birches
The mockingbirds sing lucidly.
A soft sun shines. A blue jay perches
High on the knotted peppertree.
The whales move southward. Snail tracks harden
In Matt and Joan's unguarded garden,
And wrinkling unplucked olives thrive
Along the curve of Campus Drive.
Magnolias shed their vein-bruised petals.
The vineyard turns a fiery red.
In John's yard, each untended bed
Grows thick with weeds. Inside, dust settles
Through his disordered rooms. He holds
A note he stares at, then unfolds.

13.51   He hesitates a minute, eyeing
The script; then reads on. When he's done,
His chest is tight, and he is crying.
It says, *Dear John, We have a son.*
We hope that you'll be his godfather.
We've called him John. We would far rather
Have you than any other friend.
Please speak to us, John. In the end,
We'll all be old or dead or dying.
My mother died two weeks ago.
We thought perhaps you might not know.
Phil and I send our love. Liz. Sighing
A harsh, prolonged, exhausted breath,
John feels his heart revisit death.

13.52   Depleted by his pain, he slowly
         Walks to Jan's desk. What did not last
         In life has now possessed him wholly.
         Nothing can mitigate the past.
         He gently touches Jan's sand dollar.
         It soothes him in the ache, the squalor
         That is his life, and she seems near
         Him once again, and he can hear
         Her voice, can almost hear her saying,
         "I'm with you, John. You're not alone.
         Trust me, my friend; there is the phone.
         It isn't me you are obeying.
         Pay what are your own heart's arrears.
         Now clear your throat; and dry these tears."

About the Author

The author, Vikram Seth, directed
By Anne Freedgood, his editor,
To draft a vita, has selected
The following salient facts for her:
In '52, born in Calcutta.
8 lb. 1 oz. Was heard to utter
First rhymes ("cat," "mat") at age of three.
A student of demography
And economics, he has written
From Heaven Lake, a travel book
Based on a journey he once took
Through Sinkiang and Tibet. Unbitten
At last by wanderlust and rhyme,
He keeps Pacific Standard Time.